Kaizen Workshops
for Lean Healthcare

Kaizen Workshops for Lean Healthcare

Rona Consulting Group & Productivity Press

Thomas L. Jackson, Editor

CRC Press
Taylor & Francis Group
Boca Raton London New York

CRC Press is an imprint of the
Taylor & Francis Group, an **informa** business

A PRODUCTIVITY PRESS BOOK

CRC Press
Taylor & Francis Group
6000 Broken Sound Parkway NW, Suite 300
Boca Raton, FL 33487-2742

© 2013 by Taylor & Francis Group, LLC
CRC Press is an imprint of Taylor & Francis Group, an Informa business

No claim to original U.S. Government works

Printed in the United States of America on acid-free paper
Version Date: 20120615

International Standard Book Number: 978-1-4398-4152-5 (Paperback)

Visit the Taylor & Francis Web site at
http://www.taylorandfrancis.com

and the CRC Press Web site at
http://www.crcpress.com

Contents

Preface

Kaizen means, simply, *continuous improvement.* It is based on the fundamentals of scientific analysis in which you analyze (take apart) the elements of a process or system to understand how it works so that you can learn how to influence it (make it better). Kaizen is the building block of all the Lean healthcare methodologies; it is the foundation upon which all of these methods have been built. The small, gradual, incremental changes of continuous improvement applied over a long period add up to major positive impacts on patients' access to healthcare, patient safety, and the quality of medical results.

Once your healthcare organization has committed to supporting a culture of continuous improvement, kaizen workshops can be held periodically to make focused changes in the workplace. These workshops will take a magnifying glass, so to speak, to each process and every operation in the medical center in order to eliminate waste and improve services.

This book was written to take you through the steps of conducting a very effective kaizen workshop—one that is well planned, well implemented, and well monitored after said changes are implemented. The information is presented in a highly organized and easy-to-assimilate format. Numerous illustrations reinforce the text, and margin assists call your attention to key points and other important features. Throughout the book, you are asked to reflect on questions that will help you apply these concepts and techniques to your own workplace. Each chapter has a summary for quick review.

Chapter 1 helps you get started by suggesting strategies for reading and learning, explains the instructional format of the book, and provides an overview of each chapter. Chapter 2 defines the key concepts and explores the elements of the "production" of healthcare services. It also explains the key differences between healthcare processes and the individual operations or cycles of work that processes link together. Chapters 3 and 4 provide foundational information for kaizen and kaizen workshops and explain the key roles for success. Chapter 5 explains planning and preparation, and Chapter 6 covers implementation. Chapter 7 includes examples of how to present your workshop results to the organization and how to follow up. It is through good follow-up that you reap full benefits from kaizen. Chapter 8 presents a concise summary of kaizen workshop steps. Finally, the Appendix provides a list of additional resources for learning more about the kinds of improvement methodologies you might want to implement with kaizen workshops.

If your healthcare organization fully applies the steps in this book to conducting kaizen workshops, it will gain much more than the knowledge of how to conduct a workshop. Through kaizen, employees are empowered and encouraged to make positive changes. Because they will practice working in teams, the organization will reap the synergy that comes from a collective focus on improvement. And incrementally, kaizen workshops will become more than isolated events—they will become the way all work is done.

Acknowledgments

The development of *Kaizen for Lean Healthcare* has been a team effort. In particular, I would like to thank Susie Creger, Erin Ressler, Ann Kernan, Rona Consulting Group consultants and former team members of the Virginia Mason Kaizen Promotion Office, for expertly educating and coaching the senior leaders of our healthcare clients on how to run a good kaizen workshop. Thanks also to all of the Rona Consulting Group consultants who have contributed to our workshop standard work. A lot happens in the course of five days, especially when your improvement team is top heavy with talented doctors and nurses. Thank you for helping our clients (and me personally) keep track of it all. Finally, I would also like to thank the many talented people of the Productivity Press Development Team, especially Judith Allen, who created the original book, *Kaizen for the Shop Floor*, upon which this book is based.

We are very pleased to bring you this addition to our Lean Tools for Healthcare Series and wish you continued and increasing success on your Lean journey.

Thomas L. Jackson, Series Editor

Chapter 1

Getting Started

1.1 PURPOSE OF THIS BOOK

Kaizen for Lean Healthcare was written to give you the information you need to participate in implementing this important Lean healthcare approach in your workplace. You are a valued member of your healthcare organization's transformation team; your knowledge, support, and participation are necessary to the success of any major improvement effort in your organization.

You may be reading this book because your team leader or manager asked you to do so. Or you may be reading it because you think it will provide information that will help you in your work. By the time you finish Chapter 1, you will have a better idea of how the information in this book can help you and your healthcare organization eliminate waste and serve your patients more effectively.

1.2 WHAT THIS BOOK IS BASED ON

This book is about kaizen, a critical tool for implementing Lean healthcare services and eliminating waste from healthcare processes. Kaizen is a methodology of continuous, incremental improvement. Kaizen workshops are used to bring quick and focused improvements and make significant changes in the way processes work and areas function. The methods and goals discussed in this book support the Lean healthcare system developed at Toyota Motor Company. Since 1979, Productivity Press has published information about these approaches. Since 2007, Rona Consulting Group has been applying the knowledge on the shop floor of healthcare. Today, top organizations around the world are applying Lean healthcare principles to improve patient safety and make healthcare more affordable.

Kaizen for Lean Healthcare draws on a wide variety of resources. Its aim is to present the main concepts and steps of running kaizen workshops in a simple, illustrated format that is easy to read and understand.

1.3 TWO WAYS TO USE THIS BOOK

There are at least two ways to use this book:

1. As reading material for a learning group or study group process within your organization
2. For learning on your own

Your organization may decide to design its own learning group process based on *Kaizen for Lean Healthcare.* Alternatively, you may read this book for individual learning without formal group discussion. Either way, you will learn valuable concepts and methods to apply to your daily work.

1.4 HOW TO GET THE MOST OUT OF YOUR READING

1.4.1 Become Familiar with This Book as a Whole

There are a few steps you can follow to make it easier to absorb the information in this book. Take as much time as you need to become familiar with the material. First, get a "big picture" view of the book by doing the following:

How-to Steps

- Scan the Table of Contents to see how *Kaizen for Lean Healthcare* is arranged.
- Read the rest of this introductory section for an overview of the book's contents.
- Flip through the book to get a feel for its style, flow, and design. Notice how the chapters are structured and glance at the illustrations.

1.4.2 Become Familiar with Each Chapter

After you have a sense of the overall structure of *Kaizen for Lean Healthcare,* prepare yourself to study one chapter at a time. For each chapter, we suggest you follow these steps to get the most out of your reading:

How-to Steps

- Flip through the chapter, looking at the way it is laid out. Notice the bold headings and the key points flagged in the margins.
- Now read the chapter. How long this takes depends on what you already know about the content and what you are trying to get out of your reading. Enhance your reading by doing the following:
  - Use the margin assists to help you follow the flow of information.
  - If the book is your own, use a highlighter to mark key information and answers to your questions about the material. If the book is not your own, take notes on a separate piece of paper.
  - Answer the Take Five questions in the text. These will help you absorb the information by reflecting on how you might apply it to your own workplace.
- Read the Summary at the end of the chapter to reinforce what you have learned. If you read something in the Summary that you don't remember, find that section in the chapter and review it.
- Finally, read the Reflections questions at the end of the chapter. Think about these questions and write down your answers.

1.4.3 How a Reading Strategy Works

When reading a book, many people think they should start with the first word and read straight through until the end. This is not usually the best way to learn from a book. The steps just suggested for how to read this book are a strategy for making your reading easier, more fun, and more effective.

Reading strategy is based on two simple points about the way people learn. The first point is this: *It's difficult for your brain to absorb new information if it does not have a structure to place it in.* As an analogy, imagine trying to build a house without first putting up a framework.

Like building a frame for a house, you can give your brain a framework for the new information in the book by getting an overview of the contents and then flipping through the material. Within each chapter, you repeat this process on a smaller scale by reading the key points and headings before reading the text.

The second point about learning is this: *It is a lot easier to learn if you take in the information one layer at a time, instead of trying to absorb it all at once.* It's like painting the walls of a house: First you lay down a coat of primer. When that is dry, you apply a coat of paint, and later a finish coat.

1.4.4 Using the Margin Assists

As you've noticed by now, this book uses small images called *margin assists* to help you follow the information in each chapter. There are seven types of margin assists:

1. Background Information: Sets the stage for what comes next

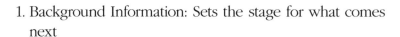

2. Definition: Defines how the author uses key terms

3. Key Point: Highlights important ideas to remember

4. Example: Helps you understand the key points

5. New Tool: Helps you apply what you have learned

6. How-to Steps: Gives you a set of directions for using new tools

7. Principle: Explains how things work in a variety of situations

1.5 AN OVERVIEW OF THE CONTENTS

1.5.1 Chapter 1: Getting Started

This chapter has already explained the purpose of *Kaizen for Lean Healthcare* and how it was written. Then it shared tips for getting the most out of your reading. It will now give a brief description of each chapter.

1.5.2 Chapter 2: Production Processes and Operations of Healthcare

Chapter 2 describes the industrial origins of the Lean healthcare methodology and explains the critical distinction between healthcare processes and healthcare operations.

1.5.3 Chapter 3: What Is Kaizen?

Chapter 3 introduces and defines kaizen and its purpose for the workplace. The concepts of *value, value-added,* and *waste* are defined in relation to kaizen. This chapter also discusses what is needed to be successful in implementing kaizen and explains how kaizen and kaizen workshops benefit both healthcare organizations and their employees.

1.5.4 Chapter 4: What Is a Kaizen Workshop and What Are the Key Roles for Success?

Chapter 4 describes a kaizen workshop and the key roles people must play for kaizen workshops to be successful. Cautions about running kaizen workshops are explained, including an example based upon experiences at both Park Nicollet Health Services in Minneapolis, Minnesota, and the Virginia Mason Medical Center in Seattle, Washington. The role of communication in a successful workshop is discussed and the three phases of a workshop are introduced.

1.5.5 Chapter 5: Phase One: Plan and Prepare

Chapter 5 highlights the key steps in preparing for a kaizen workshop. It describes how to select an area and choose an improvement focus. An important discussion about identifying waste is included. How to select the leader and team, and how to prepare the area for the kaizen workshop are explained. Details about the team leader's role and tools for the team leader are provided. The chapter concludes with information about scheduling the workshop.

1.5.6 Chapter 6: Phase Two: Run the Kaizen Workshop

Chapter 6 describes the details involved in running the workshop and provides valuable documents to be used during workshop activities. How to understand the current situation and how to begin improvements—developing improvement ideas, implementing new plans, testing improvement ideas, and developing new standards—are all explained.

1.5.7 Chapter 7: Phase Three: Report and Follow-Up

Chapter 7 discusses the final phase where results of the kaizen workshop are presented to the entire medical center. Follow-up steps must be developed to ensure that the improvements become new standards of operation. A brief celebration can be planned to congratulate the team.

1.5.8 Chapter 8: Reflections and Conclusions

Chapter 8 reflects on and presents a conclusion to this book. It includes an implementation summary for conducting a kaizen workshop.

Chapter 2

Production Processes and Operations of Healthcare

2.1 INDUSTRIAL ORIGINS OF LEAN HEALTHCARE

The purpose of the *Lean Tools for Healthcare* Series is to introduce readers to a set of methods that have been proven to dramatically increase patient safety and reduce the cost of providing healthcare services. The term *Lean* was coined to express the notion that, like an athlete, an organization should be without organizational "fat," or what Lean specialists refer to as *non-value-adding waste*, where *value* refers to what a patient would be willing to pay for. Figure 2.1 lists seven distinct types of waste found in healthcare.

BACKGROUND INFO

Lean tools and methods have important origins in the United States but were perfected principally within the Toyota Motor Company between 1948 and 1963, and have since been copied by most sectors of the manufacturing industry. The first major implementation in the healthcare industry began in 2001, when the Virginia Mason Medical Center in Seattle, Washington, engaged consultants (most of whom had been production engineers from Toyota and the Boeing Aircraft Company) to teach them how to apply the Toyota Production System to the production of healthcare services. A few years later, another major implementation was launched by

The Seven Major Categories of Healthcare Waste

Definitions	Clinical Wastes	Administrative Wastes
1. Excess production		
Producing more, sooner, or faster than is required by the next process	Unnecessary tests or labs Unnecessary medicines Unnecessary surgeries	"Copy all" emails Too many reports Too many meetings Extra copies
2. Waiting		
Time delays, process idle time	Waiting for lab results Waiting for doctors Waiting for nurses Waiting for patients	Waiting for information system response Waiting for approvals
3. Transport		
Unnecessary handling or transportation; multiple handling	Too many patient transfers Transport of equipment	Transport of paper medical records Transferring data files between incompatible information systems
4. Excess processing		
Unnecessary processing, steps, or work elements or procedures	Asking the patient the same question 20 times Multiple entries of same information in patient charts	Long meetings Long reports Reentering data Reformatting presentations
5. Excess inventory		
Producing, holding, or purchasing unnecessary inventory	Patients waiting Too many supplies Too many prosthetic devices Doctor's favorite supplies	Decisions in process Too much information Too many forms
6. Excess movement		
Excessive handling, unnecessary steps, nonergonomic motion	Walking all day Standing all day Lifting more than 35 pounds Reaching, bending, twisting	Sitting all day Walking back and forth to printers, copiers, fax machines Reaching, bending, twisting
7. Defects		
Rework, correction of errors, quality problems, equipment problems	Hospital-acquired infections Wrong meds Wrong-side surgeries Wrong patient Expired supplies Patient returns	Order-entry errors Invoice errors Outdated information Outdated forms

Figure 2.1 The seven wastes. (Reprinted with permission. J. Michael Rona and Associates, LLC, doing business as Rona Consulting Group © 2008–2012, http://www.ronaconsulting.com. All rights reserved.)

Park Nicollet Health Services in Minneapolis, Minnesota, and a few other organizations, including Thedacare in Wisconsin. The success of these implementations is well documented.*

Naturally, readers coming to the subject of *Lean health-care* for the first time are often perplexed by the patently industrial point of view taken by Lean healthcare specialists. How can healthcare be treated as an industrial process? Isn't medicine an art? Can healthcare processes be standardized when all patients are unique? In fact, medicine and health-care practice are generally becoming more scientific or evidence based, and the Center for Medicare and Medicaid Services (CMS) and deeming authorities such as the Joint Commission are quick to require adherence to standard-ized, evidence-based practices. Moreover, industrial engi-neering has long been applied to healthcare processes. Some readers may recall actor Clifton Web's portrayal of the time-and-motion consultant Frank Gilbreth in the movie, *Cheaper by the Dozen*. The movie depicts Gilbreth's ground-breaking time and motion studies of surgery in hospital operating rooms. In many ways, the practice of Lean health-care continues in the tradition of Gilbreth's time studies. The major difference is that the studies are not carried out by consultants; the studies are conducted by members of the healthcare team (clinicians and support staff), frequently with the voluntary participation of patients themselves.

2.2 PRODUCTION, PROCESS, AND OPERATION

Before studying Lean healthcare, you must understand pre-cisely how the notion of *production* applies to the production of healthcare services.† As perplexing as it may seem, produc-tion is not necessarily an activity that requires machines.

---

* John Black with David Miller, The Toyota Way to Healthcare Excellence: Increase Efficiency and Improve Quality with Lean (Chicago: Health Administration Press, 2008).

† Much of this chapter paraphrases, in language friendly to healthcare, Chapter 1 of Shigeo Shingo's groundbreaking book, *A Study of the Toyota Production System from an Industrial Engineering Perspective* (Cambridge, MA: Productivity Press, 1989).

Production is the making of either a product or a service—it doesn't matter which. Obviously, artisans produced goods and services before the advent of steam power. In its most general sense, production is simply a network of what industrial engineers call processes and operations.

A *process* is a sequence of cycles of work called operations. An *operation* is a work cycle defined by a sequence of specific tasks.

Figure 2.2 illustrates how a healthcare process—transforming a patient from the state of *unhealthy* to *healthy*—is accomplished through a series of medical and other healthcare operations. When we look at a healthcare process over time (especially when we see it from the patient's perspective), we see flows of patients, clinicians, medicines, supplies, equipment, and information in time and space. We see the transformation of the patient from the moment at which he or she presents undiagnosed symptoms, to initial assessment, definitive diagnosis, and finally treatment and recovery. When we look at operations, on the other hand, we see the work performed by doctors, nurses, lab technicians, pharmacists, and others, to accomplish this transformation—the interaction of patients, clinicians, medications, information, supplies, and equipment in time and space.

To make fundamental improvement in the process of producing healthcare services, we must distinguish the flow of patients (process) from the clinical work flow (operation) and analyze them separately. This is why in Figure 2.2 we have illustrated healthcare production as a network of processes and operations. The analysis of healthcare *processes* examines the flow of patients; the analysis of healthcare *operations* examines the work performed on patients by clinicians and support staff.

Consider a typical patient who makes a visit to an outpatient clinic: First, the patient is registered at the front desk and then asked to wait. Next, a medical assistant calls the patient and escorts him or her to an examination room. The medical assistant may take the patient's blood pressure and ask questions to make an initial assessment of the patient's condition. Again the patient is asked to wait until the doctor is ready. Finally, the doctor interviews the patient

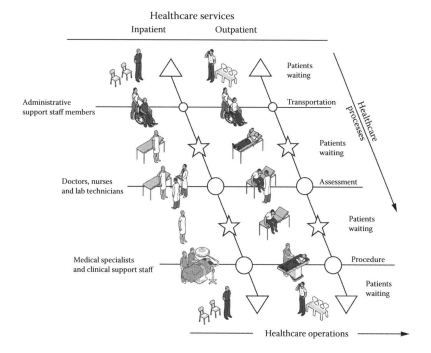

Figure 2.2 The healthcare service production process. (Reprinted with permission. J. Michael Rona and Associates, LLC, doing business as Rona Consulting Group and iStockphoto LP © 2008–2012, http://www.ronaconsulting.com; http://istockphoto.com. All rights reserved.)

and reaches a diagnosis. After this, the patient receives some treatment, let's say, an injection administered by a nurse. The nurse draws the prescribed medication, cleans the patient's injection site, and injects the medication into the patient's bloodstream. This series of changes in the patient (from undiagnosed to treated) is the *process*. The nurse's actions of filling the syringe, cleaning the patient's injection site, and injecting the medication into the patient comprise an *operation*.

2.3 SUMMARY

All production carried out in any healthcare setting—in the operating room, the clinic, the lab, or the pharmacy—must be understood as a functional network of process and operation. Healthcare *processes* transform unwell patients into well patients. Healthcare *operations* are the clinical actions that accomplish those transformations. These fundamental concepts and their relationship must be understood in order to make effective, evidence-based improvements in the production of healthcare services.

2.4 REFLECTIONS

Now that you have completed this chapter, take 5 minutes to think about these questions and write down your answers:

1. What did you learn from reading this chapter that stands out as being particularly useful or interesting to you in healthcare?
2. How do you feel about the idea of "producing" healthcare services using industrial methods?
3. Do you have any questions about the topics presented in this chapter? If so, what are they?
4. Are there any special obstacles in your mind or the minds of your colleagues to applying the distinction between process and operation in healthcare?
5. What information do you still need to fully understand the ideas presented?
6. How can you get this information?
7. Whom do you need to involve in this process?

Chapter 3

What Is Kaizen?

Key Point

In this book we will be looking closely at the roots of Lean healthcare service production, the meaning of kaizen, and the process of conducting a kaizen workshop or *blitz*, as it is sometimes called. From the start you must remember that *a kaizen workshop will fail unless it is conducted within the framework of a commitment to the philosophy of kaizen itself.* First, what is kaizen and why is it so important?

3.1 WHAT IS KAIZEN?

Definition

Kaizen means, simply, *continuous improvement.* In Japanese *kai* means "to take apart" and *zen* means "to make good." Together, these two words mean to take something apart in order to make it better. Kaizen is based on the fundamentals of scientific analysis in which you analyze (or take apart) the elements of a process or system to understand how it works, and then discover how to influence or improve it (make it better).

Lean healthcare service production is founded on the idea of kaizen. In practice, kaizen depends on fast cycles of learning and application based upon the scientific method, in the form of the *Deming Cycle:*

- *Plan:* Observe and then develop a new vision.
- *Do:* Implement rapidly to test the idea.
- *Check:* Check the results.
- *Act:* Develop awareness; a change in thinking.

These cycles of learning, applied over a long period of time, add up to a major impact on healthcare operations and results (see Figure 3.1).

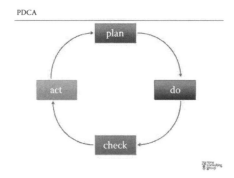

Figure 3.1   The Plan-Do-Check-Act (PDCA) cycle.

3.1.1 Kaizen and Kaikaku

Broadly speaking, kaizen refers to two types of managed change: kaizen and kaikaku. Technically speaking, kaizen refers specifically to the continuous, incremental improvement of standard work on the front line of Lean healthcare operations. In broad terms, however, kaizen also refers to *kaikaku*, the major or radical change that is linked to your organization's strategy by means of formal proposals called A3s (see Figure 3.2). Both types of change are generally referred to as kaizen.

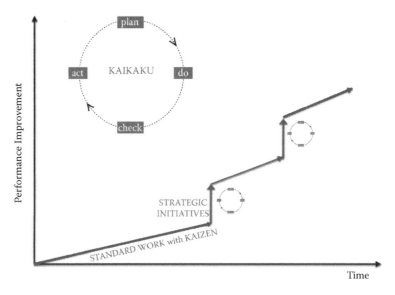

Figure 3.2   Kaizen (continuous improvement) and kaikaku (radical improvement) work in tandem to improve performance over time.

14

Ten Basic Principles for Improvement

1. Throw out all of your fixed ideas about how to do things.

2. Think of how the new method will work—not how it won't.

3. Don't accept excuses. Challenge the status quo.

4. Don't seek perfection. A 50-percent implementation rate is fine as long as it's done on the spot.

5. Correct mistakes the moment they're found.

6. Don't spend a lot of money on improvements. Think: Low cost/no cost.

7. Problems give you a chance to use your brain.

8. Ask "Why?" at least five times until you find the ultimate cause.

9. Ten people's ideas are better than one person's.

10. Improvement knows no limits.

Figure 3.3   The right spirit of kaizen.

3.1.2 What Do You Need to Know to Fully Understand How to Do Kaizen?

Key Point

The main thing you need to know to begin a continuous improvement program is how important it is—how the smallest ideas can lead to the greatest results. Kaizen is the building block of all the Lean healthcare service production methodologies; it is the foundation upon which all these methods have been built. The ten principles for improvement shown in Figure 3.3 describe the spirit you need to have in order to be successful in your kaizen activities. These will be discussed throughout the book.

TAKE FIVE

Take five minutes to think about these questions and to write down your answers:

1. What continuous improvement activities have you done in your healthcare organization?
2. Can you think of one thing you could change that would improve the way you perform your operation?

3.1.3 How Will Kaizen Change What You Are Doing Now?

If your medical center has not been doing continuous improvement, this will be a big change for you in many ways. You will need time to think about what you do, and time to learn and discover ways to do what you do better. You will need tools to help you remember your ideas. In the beginning, just jotting down ideas on cards or a notepad that fits in your pocket is all you will need. As kaizen grows in your workplace, you will learn more and more methods to help you understand your work, the equipment and instruments you use, and the relationship of your work to everyone else's in the *value stream*.

The *value stream* is all the activities in your healthcare organization that are needed to organize and produce a treatment or service and deliver it safely to your patient. As you commit to a kaizen approach, you will be *adding value* and *reducing waste* in the value stream. Figure 3.4 shows a simple value stream map for a healthcare service.

3.2 WHAT IS THE PURPOSE OF KAIZEN?

Kaizen activities focus on each *process* and every *operation* in order to add *value* and eliminate *waste*. Let's take a minute to review these terms.

3.2.1 Process and Operation

As discussed in Chapter 2, a *process* is a sequence of cycles of work, called *operations*, needed to produce and deliver a treatment or healthcare service to a patient—to transform a patient from the state of *unhealthy* to *healthy*. It includes the people, equipment, supplies, and methods used.

An *operation* is *a work cycle* defined by a sequence of specific tasks.

3.2.2 Value and Value-Added

Value is the worth of a healthcare treatment or service or related product such as medicines or medical devices delivered

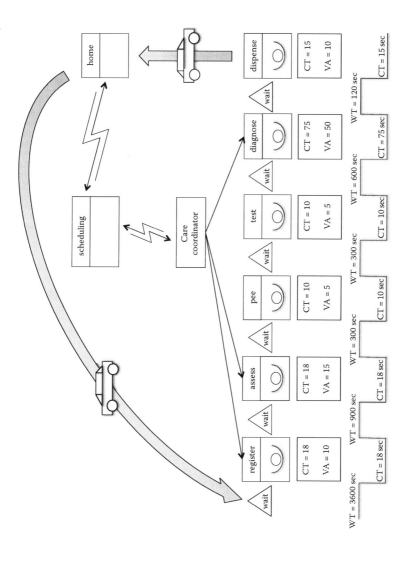

Figure 3.4 A sample value stream map. WT = Wait Time; VA = Value Added Time; and CT = Cycle Time

to a patient. It is the degree to which a patient requirement, need, or desire is fulfilled and may include quality, usefulness, functionality, availability, price, attractiveness, and so on.

Value-added refers to any operation in a healthcare process that changes information about the patient, medical know-how, medicines, and supplies into value for the patient.

3.2.3 Waste

Waste is any operation that adds cost or time but does not add value. The key to Lean healthcare service production is the total elimination of waste.

There are seven basic types of waste that have been identified by the creators of the Toyota Production System:

1. *Overproduction* or *excess production* is producing more, sooner, or faster than the patient requires.
2. *Waiting* is process idle time and time delays before the next process step begins.
3. *Transport* is unnecessary or multiple handling or movement of supplies, patients, or equipment.
4. *Overprocessing* or *excess processing* is unnecessary steps, work elements, or procedures.
5. *Inventory* or *excess inventory* is producing, holding, or purchasing unnecessary supplies or equipment.
6. *Motion* or *excess movement* is unnecessary reaching, walking, or looking for patients, instruments, records, or information.
7. *Defects* are rework and correction of errors, quality problems, and equipment problems.

The primary purpose of kaizen and Lean healthcare service production is to eliminate these forms of waste in the healthcare service production process.

As you think carefully about your own work and how to improve it, you will start to become more aware that what you do impacts what others do, and what others do impacts you. At this point, your supervisor or manager can begin small group

continuous improvement activities. *Continuous improvement*

Figure 3.5 A kaizen team solving a problem.

TAKE FIVE

Take five minutes to think about these questions and to write down your answers:

1. What operation(s) are you responsible for in your healthcare process?
2. What do you do that is value-added?
3. What is the purpose of kaizen?

---

teams are the cornerstone of kaizen and Lean healthcare service production. In teams of clinicians and staff members, you can help each other identify problems in your operations and the processes you perform together. You can share with one another what you need from each other and discover better ways of working together. Eventually, you can participate as teams in kaizen workshops or blitzes to change the layout of your work area and make improvements that affect more than just one individual and his or her workstation (see Figure 3.5).

3.3 WHAT IS THE ROLE OF A KAIZEN WORKSHOP?

Once the commitment to kaizen is made, kaizen workshops or blitzes can be held periodically to make focused changes in the workplace that affect the whole team simultaneously. A kaizen workshop must be carefully prepared, well coordinated, and thoroughly followed-up in order to be successful. The rest of this book will describe how to carry out a successful kaizen workshop.

3.4 BENEFITS OF KAIZEN AND KAIZEN WORKSHOPS

3.4.1 How Does Kaizen Benefit Your Healthcare Organization?

1. Kaizen eliminates the hidden costs that result from the seven types of waste that can exist in the healthcare service production process.
2. Kaizen improves the value-added operations in the healthcare service production process so that the service delivered to the patient is of the highest quality, lowest cost, and shortest delivery time possible.
3. A kaizen workshop allows major changes to be made in particular areas quickly and with minimum loss of healthcare service production time.

3.4.2 How Does Kaizen Benefit You?

1. Kaizen helps you eliminate wasted motion and delays in your work so that you can do what you do best with ease and without annoying interruptions.
2. Kaizen provides methods for you to think about what you do and contribute ideas that benefit the whole healthcare organization.
3. A kaizen workshop provides the opportunity to work with your teammates to improve your working environment together.

3.5 SUMMARY

A kaizen workshop will fail unless it is conducted within the framework of a commitment to the philosophy of kaizen itself. Kaizen means, simply, *continuous improvement,* and in practice also refers to *kaikaku,* which mean *major or radical change.* Kaizen is based on the fundamentals of scientific analysis in which you analyze the elements of a process or system to understand how it works, and then discover how to influence or improve it. These cycles of change are known as the Deming cycle—*Plan-Do-Check-Act.* Lean healthcare service production is founded on the idea of kaizen, upon which all of the Lean methods have been built.

If your healthcare organization has not been doing continuous improvement, this will be a big change for you in many ways. You will need time to think about what you do and learn how to discover ways to do what you do better. You will need tools to help you remember your ideas. In the beginning, just jotting down ideas on cards or a notepad that fits in your pocket is all you will need. As kaizen grows in your workplace, you will learn more and more methods to help you understand your work, the equipment and instruments you use, and the relationship of your work to everyone else's in the value stream.

The *value stream* is all the activities in your healthcare organization that are needed to produce and deliver a healthcare service to your patient. As you commit to a kaizen approach you will be *adding value* and *reducing waste* in the value stream. Kaizen activities focus on each process and every operation in order to add value and eliminate waste. A *process* is a sequence of cycles of work needed to produce and deliver a treatment or service. It includes the people, equipment, supplies, and methods used. An *operation* is a work cycle defined by a sequence of specific tasks. *Value* is the worth of a treatment or service delivered to a patient. It is the degree to which a patient need or desire is fulfilled and may include quality, usefulness, functionality, availability, price, attractiveness, and so on.

Value-added refers to any operation in a process that changes information about the patient, medical know-how, medicines, or supplies into value for the patient. *Waste* is any operation that adds cost or time but does not add value. The key to Lean healthcare service production is the total elimination of waste.

There are seven basic types of waste: overproduction, waiting, transportation, overprocessing, inventory, motion, and defects. The primary purpose of kaizen and Lean healthcare service production is to eliminate these forms of waste.

Continuous improvement teams are the cornerstone of kaizen and Lean healthcare service production. In teams of clinicians and staff members, you can identify problems and discover better ways of working together.

Once the commitment to kaizen is made, kaizen workshops or blitzes can be held periodically to make focused changes in the workplace that affect the whole team simultaneously. A kaizen workshop must be carefully prepared, well coordinated, and thoroughly followed-up in order to be successful.

3.6 REFLECTIONS

Now that you have completed this chapter, take five minutes to think about these questions and to write down your answers:

- What did you learn from reading this chapter that stands out as particularly useful or interesting?
- Do you have any questions about the topics presented in this chapter? If so, what are they?
- What additional information do you need to fully understand the ideas presented in this chapter?

Chapter 4

What Is a Kaizen Workshop and What Are the Key Roles for Success?

In the previous chapter we discussed the meaning of kaizen and the importance of an ongoing commitment to continuous improvement in the medical center before implementing a kaizen workshop. In this chapter we will define a kaizen workshop, describe some things you should be aware of before starting, identify the roles people need to play for a successful workshop, and introduce the three phases of a kaizen workshop.

4.1 WHAT IS A KAIZEN WORKSHOP?

Definition

A *kaizen workshop* is a team activity aimed at rapid use of Lean methods to eliminate waste in particular areas of the healthcare organization. It is well-planned and highly structured to enable quick, focused discovery of root causes and implementation of solutions.

How-to Steps

Before the workshop takes place, an area is selected and prepared, a problem is chosen, a baseline is determined, and an improvement target and measurements are established. Leaders and teams are selected and trained, and a time frame for the workshop is set.

Kaizen workshops typically last five days, sometimes including late nights or early mornings, although many successful kaizen activities are planned for shorter periods—from a half day to three days. These shorter initiatives, referred to as *kaizen events,* focus more narrowly

Definition

and require less planning; they usually work well after longer kaizen workshops have achieved major breakthroughs in the selected areas, making the identification of more focused problem-solving areas possible.

Definition

Every kaizen workshop is chartered by an *A3T*, a team charter (printed on large-format paper) that links the activity clearly to a significant problem and establishes definite targets and milestones (see Figure 4.1).

4.2 HOW IS A PROBLEM SELECTED?

Key Point

Once a value stream map has been completed, major problems or opportunities for improvement within the value stream can be identified. A kaizen workshop focuses on one or more of these opportunities. Problems chosen for kaizen should be ones that cause significant pain to the organization, but can also be addressed successfully in a five-day workshop with follow-up activities.

Technically, kaizen workshops are really kaikaku events. In mature Lean enterprises, the need for kaizen workshops is determined in tandem with strategic planning, or when major, unanticipated problems occur.

Kaizen workshops can focus simply on starting 5S (a method for creating a clutter-free and organized workplace) or creating standard work in one work area, or other goals limited to reducing waste in a single area or operation; or they can focus on rearranging the layout of an entire process. The more challenging or widespread the kaizen workshop's focus, the more planning and communication will be needed for it to succeed.

4.3 CAUTIONS

Key Point

Kaizen should be done without spending new money, adding new full-time employees, or adding new equipment. Kaizen activity focuses on testing small changes that can have an *immediate* impact on access to care, patient safety, and employee satisfaction. Requests to spend large sums of money often take months for healthcare organizations to process!

Kaizen is about changing the way we think about our work *today* so that we can do it better *tomorrow*. Besides, the disarmingly simple solutions discovered during five days of a kaizen workshop frequently make adding new people or technology completely unnecessary.

There are several other issues to be aware of in using kaizen workshops to implement Lean healthcare service production.

4.3.1 Plan in Advance for Coverage

Be sure that you have adequate staff and equipment to cover the reductions that will occur during the workshop. Healthcare service production output can be affected during a workshop as clinicians and staff members direct their time to workshop activities. Sometimes stoppages are required to make significant changes in the process or layout. You will also have to retrain clinicians and staff members in new processes as these processes become established. Planning for this slowdown will ensure that overall healthcare service does not suffer while improvements become the new operation standards.

4.3.2 Put the Focus on Clinician and Staff Member Participation

Be sure, if outside consultants are used, that they do not impose their ideas on clinicians and staff but rather involve the team in creating solutions. Remember, the people who know the most about how to improve the job are the ones who do it every day. Employee training is another necessity. For clinicians and staff members to succeed in the new methods, and understand how to think about their jobs using Lean principles, they need to learn what these methods and principles are. It is not enough that the person leading the workshop understands them. Everyone involved must be trained.

Park Nicollet Health Services provides healthcare services to millions of people in the Minneapolis, Minnesota area and is a pioneer in Lean healthcare management. The story

A3-T

Proposed team charter	Theme: Focus on the process to achieve results

PROBLEM STATEMENT

In 2010, the organization produced $____ in Earnings Before Sustaining Cost, or a contribution margin of ____%. The organization is forecast to produce $____ in EBSC in 2009; this is insufficient to meet the ____% contribution margin required to support organization's companywide financial targets, designed to address the financial risks of economic uncertainty and increased pressure to reduce the cost of healthcare.

Contribution margin

TARGET STATEMENT

By December 31, 2012, the organization will improve revenue by ____% from ____ to ____, Direct Cost by ____% from ____ to ____, and Conversion Cost by ____% from ____ to ____, resulting in Earnings Before Sustaining Cost of ____. This is equivalent to required contribution margin of ____% necessary to meet the organization's strategic financial targets for the organization as a whole.

ANALYSIS

In the next five to ten years, the Baby Boomers will become eligible for Medicare, which will negatively impact our payer mix. If we do not improve our cost structure, we will not be able to maintain profitability. The origins of the current cost crisis in healthcare are not financial; they in how we manage our customers and capabilities. In particular, customer satisfaction is low because quality is quite poor, and this contributes to higher cost in two ways. First, the costs of quality are known to grow exponentially until problems are found and fixed. Second, quality problems contribute to longer process lead times in all processes, contributing to higher conversion and sustaining costs. Poor quality negatively also affects revenue through curtailed Medicare reimbursements and lower brand equity. Finally, high turnover and poor retention contribute significantly to the cost of human resources.

Figure 4.1 A sample A3T charter.

A3-T

Proposed team charter   Theme: Focus on the process to achieve results

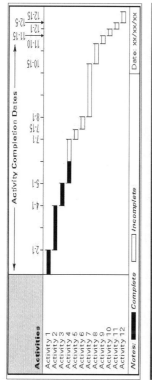

PROPOSED ACTION

It has been shown that lead-time reduction is inversely proportional to process reliability; in other words, lead-time falls as process reliability improves. Furthermore, for every 50% reduction in lead-time, unit cost should fall between 20% to 30%. Therefore, over the next five years, the organization will undertake a coordinated series of investments in quality, process reliability, and growth. In the area of customer satisfaction, we will invest in a standardized, companywide problem solving methodology. In the area of process improvement, we will strive to reduce all critical process lead times by 50%. In the area of growth, we will dedicate 5% of our staff full-time to process improvement and train 100% of our workforce in the basics of lean enterprise and in the PDCA3 problem solving process.

IMPLEMENTATION PLAN

CHECK AND ACT (verification and follow up)

Progress toward our targets will be checked frequently on the shop floor through the systematic adoption of visual management systems and daily stand-up meetings. In addition, site managers will conduct weekly standup visual reviews with all managers in attendance. Furthermore, the President's Diagnosis will be implemented, based upon the Transformation Ruler. Monthly local self-audits will be conducted. Once a year, the CEO and President will conduct a formal diagnosis and make visits to each site.

Figure 4.1 (continued)

27

of Park Nicollet provides a good example of how best to use kaizen workshops.

Before the adoption of Lean healthcare and kaizen, when the medical center was in crisis as the result of a medical error or sentinel event, they created a team of internal consultants to change the medical center using a variety of promising but piecemeal approaches to healthcare safety and quality. The quality department and Park Nicollet's leaders decided what was to be done and imposed new standards on clinicians and staff members, often to comply with explicit demands from the Center for Medicare and Medicaid Services (CMS) or the Joint Commission, Park Nicollet's deeming agency. There was little preparation before the workshops and almost no follow-up after them. While CMS and the Joint Commission might be satisfied in the short term with the actions taken, in the long term the changes did not last and the medical center was left in greater chaos than before (see Figure 4.2). In addition to the original problems, they now had a problem with morale.

In an attempt to become more systematic in its approach to change, Park Nicollet brought in experienced external quality

Figure 4.2 The kaizen blitz: Who is it for? (Reprinted with permission, J. Michael Rona and Associates, LLC, and iStockphoto LP. © 2008–2012, http://www.ronaconsulting.com and, http://istockphoto.com; All rights reserved)

consultants who helped determine the right problems on which to focus in a series of major improvement initiatives. Large numbers of internal consultants were trained in problem solving and advanced statistical methods and then put in charge of collecting and analyzing quantitative data and getting results. The emphasis was often placed first on financial improvement, not patient safety or quality. While the approach was intellectually rigorous, it depended principally upon experts, and often ignored the know-how, observations, and stories of clinicians and staff on the front line of healthcare operations. Employees still felt that the new processes and standards were being imposed on them from outside, which they were.

Key Point

The medical center shifted its improvement policy away from the expert-driven, project-based approach that imposed changes on clinicians and staff members by creating a Kaizen Promotion Office staffed by internal consultants trained in Lean healthcare and kaizen. The Kaizen Promotion Office (KPO) was an internally led system for training and empowering clinicians and staff members to make changes themselves. Park Nicollet recognized the need for outside help from experts who understood Lean healthcare service production methods and how to implement them, but now the expertise of people on the medical center floor could no longer be ignored. Many of the ideas that had been imposed on the clinicians and staff members by the quality department and external consultants were ideas the clinicians and staff members had already asked leadership to implement long before. Clinicians and staff just needed the opportunity to do what they knew should be done all along, but not by having ideas stuffed down their throats without preparation, and in a cookie-cutter approach that did not take into account the many different situations and people doing the work.

As you shift to Lean healthcare service production, it is essential that you do so *with* the people, not *to* the people. The results will be much more complete, they will last much longer, and improvements will continue to evolve because everyone doing the work will be trained and empowered to think better about their work.

4.3.3 Understand the Importance of Preparation and Follow-Up

In addition to planning for coverage and putting the focus on clinician and staff member participation, preparation and follow-up are the other cornerstones of successful kaizen workshops. You may find that preparation and follow-up require more time than conducting the workshop itself. This book provides tools for the preparation and follow-up stages. Also, the Appendix refers you to books that explain the Lean training programs you need to put in place to achieve Lean healthcare service production with kaizen workshops.

Example

At a major medical center in the Pacific Northwest, training top managers and making sure that kaizen efforts were supported for the long term from the top was the first important step the organization took after kaizen workshops failed to produce the needed results. At this point, everyone understood that the whole infrastructure had to support the shift to Lean and that the effort must be systemwide and enduring, not just something imposed during a weeklong kaizen

Key Point

workshop. This is the most critical point to know—*kaizen workshops will only succeed when done within the context of an existing culture that supports continuous improvement.*

4.4 SUCCESSFUL KAIZEN IN ACTION

Example

Figure 4.3 shows the *before* and *after* of how a series of kaizen workshops, facilitated by a healthcare organization's KPO and led by certified workshop leaders and team leaders, improved clinical flow in the organization's outpatient clinics. Prior to kaizen, the clinical flow was full of wasted motion and constant interruptions. Nurses and medical assistants walked repeatedly to and from the supply room for necessary supplies. In their offices, doctors were sometimes unaware that patients had been roomed and were waiting to see them. Despite the fact that appointments were scheduled, there did not seem to be a clear way to prioritize the work. As a result of all of these interruptions, inefficiencies, and delays, doctors frequently stayed late to chart and to respond to a multitude of requests, for example,

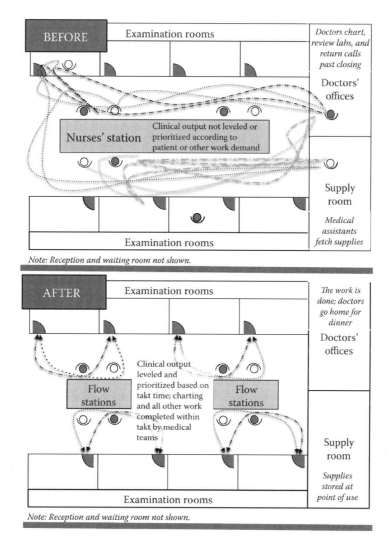

Figure 4.3 Clinical flow before and after kaizen.

from the lab and pharmacy. Doctors rarely returned home for dinner, which was a key dissatisfier for doctors, nurses, and staff alike. Not surprisingly, these clinics were losing money.

During a five-day workshop, the kaizen team decided to try something new. A doctor and a medical assistant would form a team responsible for seeing patients in two contiguous rooms, or a *healthcare production cell*. This would minimize the motion waste of walking, among other things. While the doctor saw one patient, the medical assistant would discharge the previous patient and room the next. After rooming, the medical assistant "leveled" the doctor's work by prioritizing the doctor's phone calls, charting, and requests from the lab and pharmacy and placed the necessary paperwork as kanban, or signals, in a *flow station*. The flow station, placed strategically between the two rooms, minimized walking, but mainly was used to remind the doctor that he or she had important work to do. By adopting the concepts of U-shaped production cells and leveling, the organization was able to see patients according to *takt time* (the rate of patient demand). As a result of creating this compact flow and carefully organizing all of the doctors' work, patients were seen promptly, and doctors normally completed everything before the clinic's normal closing hours and got home in time for dinner. In addition, the clinics began to turn a profit.

This groundbreaking healthcare redesign is still sustained today and has spread to other healthcare organizations. But it could not have been sustained or faithfully replicated with an expert-driven project-based approach to improvement. It is the result of Lean concepts and tools applied in the five-day kaizen workshop format described in this book, actively supported by senior leaders who themselves have been certified as workshop leaders.

4.5 WHAT ARE THE KEY ROLES FOR A SUCCESSFUL KAIZEN WORKSHOP?

There are five major roles in a kaizen team (see Figure 4.4):

1. Sponsor
2. Process owner
3. Workshop leader
4. Team leader
5. Team member

There are a number of important things to consider in determining the people who will be involved in making your kaizen workshop a success. Of course, the team members and team leader are the primary participants. Details on their roles and how to select them will be discussed in the next chapter. But there are many others whose roles will provide

Roles and responsibilities

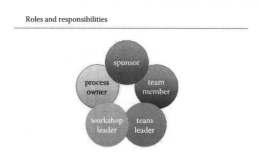

Figure 4.4   The five major roles on a kaizen team.

the backup and follow-through that the team will need before, during, and after the workshop so that their efforts take hold and bring measurable and lasting results. In addition to the five major roles, unions also provide important support for kaizen. Everyone involved will need a genuine commitment to Lean healthcare to make the kaizen workshop return optimal improvements to the medical center.

4.5.1 Workshop Leader

Key Point

The workshop leader is the highest-ranking person in the actual workshop, and the primary link (along with the team leader) between top management and the team. The workshop leader makes decisions, assignments, justifies expenditures, and coordinates all behind-the-scenes activities not handled by the team leader. He or she works with all the key players in the planning and follow-up phases to make sure the needed communication occurs. He or she should also support the process

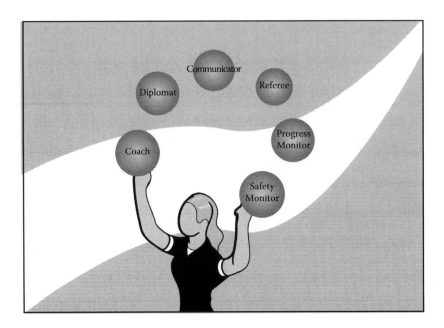

Figure 4.5 The workshop leader is a VIP with many responsibilities. (Reprinted with permission, J. Michael Rona and Associates, LLC and iStockphoto LP. © 2008–2012, http://www.ronaconsulting.com and http://istockphoto.com; All rights reserved)

owner in preparing for the workshop, and the team leader throughout the implementation (see Figure 4.5).

If you are just starting out and have never done a kaizen workshop before, you may want to use an outside professional to lead you through the first ones you do. This book is intended to provide you with many of the details involved in planning, preparing, and conducting a kaizen workshop, but once in the thick of it, you may be glad for the expertise of someone who has been there before. A consultant's primary purpose should be to educate you in Lean concepts and tools and then to help you become skilled in running these workshops so that you can do it on your own after a few experiences, and so that you can begin to train others to lead kaizen workshops. Unless an organization is doing it for itself and solutions are coming from within (not being imposed from without) the changes made in a kaizen workshop will not last nor bear long-term bottom-line results.

Key Point

Whether the workshop leader is an outside consultant or other key figure in your medical center, knowledge of kaizen workshops and experience coordinating them is essential. If trained in Lean concepts and tools and experienced with kaizen workshops, sometimes the process owner is assigned the role of workshop leader.

4.5.2 Sponsor

The sponsor decides to initiate kaizen in the medical center. (If the decision is made by an executive team, one person should be chosen to function as the sponsor.) The sponsor will choose the workshop leader (or consultant). Once kaizen is initiated, the sponsor will need to fully support the workshop leader in all their efforts to move toward Lean healthcare service production.

Kaizen is about eliminating waste in healthcare processes, not about eliminating people. Toyota succeeded with its production methods because eliminating waste led them to add production lines and increase capacity. In this way, in a very short time they dominated world markets with innovative and defect-free products. They did not eliminate workers; they eliminated costs due to waste.

One very important role of the sponsor is to make it clear throughout the healthcare organization that successfully implementing kaizen workshops and Lean processes will not endanger anyone's job. People may be reassigned, they may become kaizen team leaders and train others to lead kaizen workshops, or they may move to other work areas. Additional training will be needed for everyone when standard work and Lean healthcare operations are fully in place, and this will also ensure clinicians' and staff members' long-term value to the healthcare organization. Every team member will become more involved and empowered in improving his or her own operations.

4.5.3 The Union Role

Unions may represent some staff members, and from the start, need to be partners in the healthcare organization policy to implement Lean healthcare service production. Provisions should be added to union contracts to allow for total adoption of the methods of the Lean healthcare service production system, and this partnership should be communicated throughout the medical center. Union leaders should be included in the planning stages so that they will understand and support clinician or staff member participation in the kaizen workshop.

4.5.4 Process Owner

Key Point

The process owner, usually the department manager, works with the workshop leader (if not assigned the role of workshop leader) and participates in the planning and preparation stages: to choose an appropriate area on which to focus the workshop, to select a problem for improvement, to identify team leaders, and to guide and approve targets and measures. Neither the workshop leader nor the process owner should decide what the solutions to the targeted problems are. This is the purpose of having the workshop and is the role of the team. The people who do the job are the best ones to identify how it can be improved. However, the team members will appreciate the training and guidance provided by the process owner to help ensure their success, and will appreciate the clear understanding that the process owner and his or her superiors are fully supportive of the principles and methods of Lean healthcare service production. The process owner's primary role is to communicate wholehearted support for the kaizen teams. Knowing that the whole healthcare organization is behind you enables you to put your whole attention and best thinking into a kaizen workshop.

TAKE FIVE

Take five minutes to think about these questions and to write down your answers:

1. What is the role of the sponsor in a kaizen workshop?
2. Does your top management support Lean healthcare service production? How?
3. How does the union participate in Lean healthcare service production activities in your medical center?

4.6 COMMUNICATING TO THE WHOLE HEALTHCARE ORGANIZATION ABOUT THE KAIZEN WORKSHOP

Thorough communication will make all the difference in whether your workshop succeeds or does not. An announcement from the top will communicate serious support for the activity. Posting the schedule and a clarification of the steps will help everyone become familiar with what to expect and will reduce fears about the unknown. Daily communication about workshop progress will allow everyone to be informed and feel included, even if they are not part of the team. This will help prepare them for when they will be involved and will remove any sense of being left out of something important. Publish details as soon as they are known. Post lists of training sessions and who has completed them.

Ask the union to help communicate the details to ensure that this is a team effort. Circulate and post descriptions of what will happen during the kaizen workshop and the overall plan for workshops that will include everyone over time. Let everyone know the areas that will be affected and the benefits to be expected. Show before and after photos. At healthcare organization meetings, present video of the areas before and after the workshops. Publish photos in healthcare organization newsletters. Support departments, such as the maintenance team, will be important allies in workshops in many ways, including helping you move and reconnect equipment and providing advice about improving bottlenecks. They should be included in all memos and communications and invited to all presentations where they can be thanked publicly for their help.

Communication does not stop with the workshop itself. The formal presentation at the end of the workshop should be published, and follow-up steps should be continually posted as assignments are completed. Electronic mechanisms and physical bulletin boards should display ongoing results and future plans. Communication and visual display of kaizen efforts are important aspects of the Lean environment and should be kept updated with new information so that they become common focal points for everyone in the healthcare organization. It should be common practice for people to check the bulletin boards for new information and to look forward to having their own picture or results posted one day.

TAKE FIVE

Take five minutes to think about these questions and to write down your answers:

1. Why is communication so important to the success of a kaizen workshop?
2. Do you have a healthcare organization newsletter? Is it daily, weekly, or monthly?
3. Where is new information about goings-on at the medical center posted in your area?
4. What would you like to know more about in your medical center?

4.7 THREE PHASES OF A KAIZEN WORKSHOP

There are three primary phases of a kaizen workshop, which will be the subject of the rest of this book.

1. *Phase one:* Planning and preparation
2. *Phase two:* Implementation—the workshop itself
3. *Phase three:* Presentation and follow-up

4.8 SUMMARY

A *kaizen workshop* is a team activity aimed at rapid use of Lean methods to eliminate healthcare service production waste in particular areas of the healthcare organization. It is well-planned and highly structured to enable quick, focused discovery of root causes and implementation of solutions. Before the workshop takes place, an area is selected and prepared, a problem is chosen, a baseline is determined, and an improvement target and measurements are established. Leaders and teams are selected and trained, and a schedule is set. Workshops typically last one week, although many successful kaizen initiatives are planned for shorter periods. These shorter kaizen events focus more narrowly and less planning is required.

Kaizen workshops are chartered using an *A3T team charter* that links the workshop to a significant problem and establishes targets and milestones. Problems are usually identified after a value stream map has been completed. A workshop might focus on starting 5S or creating standard work in a single area, or on rearranging the layout of an entire process. The more challenging or widespread the kaizen workshop's focus, the more planning and communication will be needed for it to succeed.

Be sure that you have adequate staff and equipment to cover the reductions that will occur during the workshop. If outside consultants are used, be sure that they do not impose their ideas on clinicians and staff members, but rather involve the team in creating the solutions. The people who know the most about how to improve the job are the ones who do it every day. Employee training is another necessity. It is not enough that someone leading the workshop understands the methods; everyone involved must be trained.

There are a number of important things to consider in determining the people who will be involved in making your kaizen workshop a success. The team members and team leader are the primary participants, but others, including the workshop leader, sponsor, and process owner, provide support before, during, and after the workshop so that their efforts take hold and bring measurable and lasting results.

Whether the *workshop leader* is an outside consultant or other key figure in your medical center, knowledge of kaizen workshops and experience coordinating them is essential. The workshop leader is the highest-ranking person in the workshop and the primary link between top management and the team.

Kaizen is about eliminating waste in healthcare processes, not about eliminating people. One very important role of the *sponsor* is to make it clear throughout the healthcare organization that successfully implementing kaizen workshops and Lean processes will not endanger anyone's job. People may be reassigned, they may become kaizen team leaders and train others, or they may move to other areas.

Unions represent the clinicians and staff members and, from the start, need to be partners in the healthcare organization policy to implement Lean healthcare service production. *Union leaders* should be included in the planning stages so that they will understand and support employee participation in the kaizen workshop.

The process owner (if not assigned the role of workshop leader) works with the workshop leader and participates in the planning and preparation stages: to choose an appropriate area on which to focus the workshops, to select a problem for improvement, to identify team leaders, and to guide and approve targets and measures. The *process owner's* primary role is to communicate wholehearted support for the kaizen teams.

Thorough communication will make the difference in whether your workshop succeeds or does not, and it does not stop with the workshop itself. Communication and visual displays of kaizen efforts are important aspects of the Lean environment. Displays should be kept updated with new information so that they become common focal points for everyone in the healthcare organization.

There are three primary phases of a kaizen workshop: planning and preparation; implementation—the workshop itself; and the presentation and follow-up.

4.9 REFLECTIONS

Now that you have completed this chapter, take five minutes to think about these questions and to write down your answers:

- What did you learn from reading this chapter that stands out as particularly useful or interesting?
- Do you have any questions about the topics presented in this chapter? If so, what are they?
- What additional information do you need to fully understand the ideas presented in this chapter?

Chapter 5

Phase One

Plan and Prepare

In the last chapter, the importance of thorough preparation was emphasized. This chapter leads you through the key steps of preparing for a kaizen workshop. The sponsor will have given guidelines to the workshop leader as to the focus of the workshops, specific targets for process improvement, and so on. Supported by external consultants or perhaps internal consultants from a Kaizen Promotion Office, the workshop leader will be the Sensei and technical consultant to the kaizen workshop team. He or she is responsible for all three phases of the kaizen activity, including preworkshop data collection, running the workshop, and successful follow-up over a period of 90 days.

The process of planning a kaizen workshop normally begins by identifying a particular value stream that needs improvement. The workshop leader works with the process owner to prepare the value stream for the workshop and help set goals. The workshop leader and the process owner, dividing responsibilities as appropriate, schedule the workshop, select the area and the problem for improvement, and choose the team leader (or leaders, if the workshop will include more than one area).

5.1 SELECT AN AREA

How-to Steps

The first step is to choose where you will conduct your first kaizen workshop. Prior to the workshop, you will normally map value streams of interest to identify important areas that will become the focal points of kaizen activity. Kaizen activity addresses *problems in the work;* that is, problems with standard work or the lack of standard work. These are the causes of problems that result in poor performance with respect to quality, safety, cost, and delivery of healthcare services to patients.

You will want to choose an area that will have an impact but not pose too many difficult problems to solve in the beginning. Each workshop will teach you things that will make the next one smoother and easier to run successfully. Also, each workshop provides a training ground for new team leaders. As people gain experience in running workshops, and as measurable results accumulate in the areas where workshops have been run, it will become possible to tackle more complex areas and difficult problems. Start slowly and build momentum as you gain confidence and experience. You will get better each time you run a workshop and so will your teams.

You can choose several areas where you would like to start and compare the merits of each. This will ensure that you start with the best one first, based on several criteria, and help you determine what will be next. Each kaizen workshop should be chosen in order to create a progression of results that support implementation of Lean methods throughout the medical center. There are a number of things to consider as you make your choices. Use the *Kaizen Workshop Area Selection Matrix* (Figure 5.1) to help you compare criteria of different areas.

New Tool

In order to have a big impact right away, choose an area with one or more of these characteristics:

- It is deluged with work in process (WIP). (For example, in the hospital or clinic, WIP inventory consists of patients in the process. In the lab, inventory consists of lab samples.)
- It has activities that occur all over the medical center.
- It has a significant bottleneck or other major hindrance to the flow of healthcare services.
- It is an area where everything is a mess.

Kaizen Workshop Area Selection Matrix				
Criteria	Area A	Area B	Area C	Area D
Many patients waiting				
Activities occur all over the clinic or hospital				
Process bottleneck (e.g., long process setup times)				
Frequent interruptions to clinical processes				
Everything is a mess				
Medium to high patient demand or census				
No more than 12 clinicians or staff members				
Complete, not a partial process				
Multiple operations required to serve the patient				
The process is visible, robust (i.e., can deal with change)				
Process can be copied in other clinical operations or areas				
Significant market or financial impact				
Operational problems (not management issues) to resolve				
Clinicians and staff want a kaizen workshop				
Clinicians and staff have been exposed to kaizen				
Most clinicians and staff are familiar with the area				

Figure 5.1 A Kaizen Workshop Area Selection Matrix.

Do not start with highly complex areas serving a wide mix of patient needs; instead, select an area

- that has medium to high volume,
- that involves a work group of no more than twelve clinicians and staff members,
- that is a complete and not a partial process, and
- that requires four to six processes to complete the service.

The area should have a process

- that is visible,
- that is robust,
- that can be copied in other areas,
- that has significant patient or financial impact, and
- that has operational problems, not management or policy issues to resolve.

Choose an area

- where most of the clinicians and staff members are ready and willing to make changes,
- where clinicians and staff members have already been cross-trained or have been exposed to kaizen workshops before, and
- which most of the employees are familiar with.

TAKE FIVE

Take five minutes to think about these questions and to write down your answers:

1. What are five criteria for selecting an area in which to do a kaizen workshop?
2. What are three areas in your medical center that would make good kaizen starting points? Based on the Kaizen Workshop Area Selection Matrix, which of these three areas should be first and why?

5.2 SELECT A PROBLEM FOR IMPROVEMENT

How-to Steps

Once the area has been selected, the focus for the kaizen work-shop must be decided. Be sure that you clarify the boundaries of the chosen area, using the A3T charter to specify the start and end points of the process and its specific customers and suppliers. These boundaries must be maintained throughout the kaizen workshop. Talk to the people who work in the selected area about the project and work with them in decid-ing on the problem to be improved in the workshop.

The reasons you chose this particular area for a kaizen workshop probably included some understanding of what is needed in this area. Now it is time to check your assumptions and examine the conditions and the process used in this area more closely. In selecting a focus for the kaizen workshop, several things need to be considered. Has 5S been conducted there? Should that be the focus of the first workshop in this area or do you want to implement 5S more gradually before conducting the workshop?

The complexity involved and the length of time needed to prepare for your kaizen workshop depends on the problem you choose to improve or the implementation you wish to lead. These also determine the length of the workshop itself.

5.2.1 Elimination of Waste as an Overall Focus

In Chapter 3, waste was defined as any operation that adds cost or time but does not add value. Eliminating waste is the purpose and function of Lean healthcare service produc-tion. The focus of a kaizen workshop must be chosen for its impact on the waste in the selected area. Begin by examining the current state of the process in the chosen area. Analyze the process for the waste that exists there.

Key Point

You may remember the seven types of waste (see Chapter 2, Figure 2.1). *The first challenge of kaizen is to understand how to identify waste.* A good place to start is with wasted motion. Begin to examine the work you do, the operations you are responsible for, and the work area where you provide value to the patient. What gets in the way of doing your work?

Five Key Steps for Discovering Waste

---

1. Look at the three real things:
   The clinical setting
   The facts
   Patients waiting:
   - for appointments
   - for care
   - for prescriptions
   - to go home
2. Ask "What?"
   Ask *what value* the test or procedure is providing for the patient.
3. Ask "Why?"
   Ask *why* the test or procedure is necessary.
4. Everything that is not work is waste.
   Once you have found out what the test's or procedure's essential function is, you can properly identify as waste everything in the test or procedure that does not directly execute that function.
5. Ask "Why" at least 5 times to find root causes.
   Ask *why* at least 5 times concerning each wasteful part of the test or procedure. This will lead you to the real waste.

Draft an improvement plan
Ask "How"?

Figure 5.2 Five key steps for discovering waste.

When do you find yourself moving to find something you need in order to do your work? How often do you have to look for an instrument?

These questions and others like them are the start of identifying waste—looking at your own work and workplace for waste. Then you can consider how your work affects others and how others' work affects you. Begin to ask yourself these kinds of questions and you will get an idea of how kaizen works.

First you examine *what is*; you pay close attention to what you do that is value-added and what you do that is not. Five Key Steps for Discovering Waste (Figure 5.2), shows you which questions to ask to begin identifying waste. Look, without assumptions, at the area and the process to see what is really going on.

Ask: "What is the purpose?" and "Why is this necessary?" etc. Recognize what is not work in support of the primary function of the process. Ask "why" five times about each wasteful part of the operation: "Why does this occur?" "Why is this necessary?" This will lead you to the root cause of the problem and the focus of the improvement you need to make.

Key Point

Once the causes of problems are understood, you can experiment with ways to eliminate the things you do that are not value-added. *Problem solving is the heart of kaizen. It begins with one idea, and it never ends.*

Example

If you have to look for an instrument over and over again, consider why. Why does it disappear? Where do you put it when you are finished using it? Who else uses it? Where do you want it to be? When do you need it to be there? How can you make this happen? This type of problem and these questions and the solutions that will emerge as you create ideas are part of the kaizen approach called *5S*. Perhaps you have already done this in your healthcare organization. If not, a kaizen workshop can be held to get 5S started.

Are your processes chaotic or confusing so that clinicians and support staff—despite their hard work and diligence—are prone to inadvertent errors? This is all too frequently the case in healthcare. For this reason, you may want to make implementing standard work the focus of your kaizen workshop.

If you find that lengthy setup times for your clinical processes or equipment cause problems, or if you notice that

---

TAKE FIVE

Take five minutes to think about these questions and to write down your answers:

1. What are three types of waste in the operation(s) you are responsible for?
2. What are three types of waste that currently exist in your broader healthcare service department or area?
3. Can you think of one improvement idea for each waste you have identified that you would like to share with your coworkers?

you are continually moving patients for each setup you must make, you can consider learning more about quick setup techniques. But even before you advance to these methods you can do a lot on your own just by thinking about how to improve your operation by eliminating unnecessary motions.

5.3 SPECIAL CONSIDERATIONS IN CHOOSING A PROBLEM FOR IMPROVEMENT

Continuous flow, mistake-proofing, and kanban are advanced methods of Lean healthcare service production. They have grown from the simple beginning of identifying waste in order to eliminate overproduction, excess inventory, and unnecessary transport from value-added operations and processes. Kaizen workshops can focus on implementing these advanced techniques, and they are often used for this purpose, but it is wise to implement simpler approaches to identifying and eliminating waste first. Here are four special considerations related to the focus of the kaizen workshop that you choose:

1. Implementing 5S
2. Implementing standard work
3. Eliminating bottlenecks or improving setup times
4. Implementing continuous flow, mistake-proofing, or kanban

5.3.1 Implementing 5S

5S starts you off on the right foot. It's a perfect tool for bringing a team of clinicians and staff members together and allowing them to focus on their own areas first. It teaches them to focus on their own operation and identify the waste in their work without being scrutinized or criticized by others. It establishes the trust and skills needed to go the distance with Lean healthcare service production. It also puts the place in order, eliminates the "low-hanging fruit" of process waste, and establishes the discipline required to delve deeply into the process analysis needed to shift to kanban. 5S is the first step in creating a visual workplace; kanban, mistake-proofing, and continuous flow are the last steps. If you don't do 5S first, you will have to come back to it at some point.

Key Point

As a focus for a kaizen workshop, 5S makes a great first step because everyone can learn from it without risking the time and effort required to change the medical center layout entirely. (Though some equipment may need to be moved, it will probably be less disturbing to healthcare service production than shifting to continuous flow.) As 5S becomes established, process by process and area by area, everyone will see the impact of order and visual mechanisms; the medical center will start to percolate with anticipation about the possibilities of becoming a Lean healthcare facility. 5S removes so many barriers and creates such a solid foundation for the advanced *pull* methods that there need be no hesitation about choosing 5S as the focus for initial kaizen workshops.

New Tool

Use the *5S Evaluation Sheet* (Figure 5.3) to determine if you need to start with 5S before implementing other Lean healthcare service production methods. If the chosen area has an average score of less than 3.5, it would be good to start with 5S.

rona consulting group

No.	Department / Area / Zone	sort	set in order	shine	5S Level
1	Room 302	2	2	2	2
2	Room 303	2	2	3	2
2	Room 304	3	3	3	3
3	Room 305	2	2	2	2
4	Room 306	1	1	1	1

Standardization-level Summary Sheet — Assigned area: 5 South — Date: 8/2/11 — Entered by: A Kernan — Page: 1 of 1

For each area being audited, circle 3S scores as determined by the 5-point standardization checklist. The 5S level is equal to the lowest of the 3S scores.

Figure 5.3   A sample 5S Evaluation Sheet.

5.3.2 Implementing Standard Work

With 5S in place, clinicians and staff members will begin to identify inconsistencies and interruptions in their daily work. Inconsistencies and interruptions in the work of clinicians and staff members are major sources of variation, errors, and defects in healthcare and pose significant risks to patient safety. *The cure for this problem is standard work, which defines repeatable task sequences and timings to ensure that every patient receives the appropriate evidence-based care precisely when they need it.*

Key Point

By resolving conflicts among the different standards and protocols followed by various clinicians and staff, and by articulating standards where perhaps none existed—particularly in handoffs between doctors and nurses and between different departments and specialties in the healthcare system—healthcare operations are stabilized and quality and patient safety are automatically improved. Standard work creates a context for data gathering and deep problem solving and is the essential context of continuous improvement.

5.3.3 Eliminating Bottlenecks or Improving Setup Times

With 5S and standard work in place, clinicians and staff members will begin to identify additional opportunities for improvement that surface during and after the initial workshops. Particularly with respect to 5S, these opportunities may become the focus of shorter kaizen events. Meanwhile, the rollout of standard work may require consecutive workshops or, in some cases, the creation of a *model line*. Eventually, additional Lean tools are required to eliminate other non-value-adding wastes and create flow. Training in quick setup methods will help clinicians and staff members think about their operations inventively, and you will see areas of WIP inventory disappear as setup times improve. This will be the indication that you are ready to move to continuous flow and kanban.

Key Point

Be sure not to get discouraged. Wherever you start in your shift toward continuous flow, problems will arise that you didn't see before. This is the purpose of these methods. Lean healthcare is all about finding waste. The methods of Lean are brilliant in their ability to do this. Be happy—it means you are doing it right—and move quickly to remove whatever rises up to block the flow of your new process.

5.3.4 Implementing Continuous Flow, Line Balancing, or Kanban

Weeklong kaizen workshops are most often used first to stabilize the production of healthcare services through the implementation of standard work. Next, kaizen is used to transform healthcare service production lines by implementing continuous flow, supported by kanban (a card containing a sequence manufacturing specifications and requirements, used to regulate the supply of components) and pull systems. *These activities require major changes in medical center layout and complete transformation of the work standards for every process.* A great deal of planning and preparation are needed beforehand to ensure success; advance coverage must be adequate to allow the targeted operations to continue to function during the workshop, paying absolute attention to patient safety. Progress can be made workshop by workshop throughout the medical center, requiring that an organizationwide plan be made before the first workshop so that each area can switch to continuous flow logically and with the least disturbance to overall medical center effectiveness.

Key Point

It makes a great deal of sense to implement 5S and standard work throughout the medical center and remove major bottlenecks due to slow setups before attempting to install continuous flow. Many of the problems will be eliminated before requiring operations to function according to the new standards, and you will have a chance to eliminate operations that exist only because of process waste. If you shift to continuous flow before eliminating unnecessary and wasteful operations, confusion will be the result. By starting with 5S and standard work, clinicians and staff members will become used to solving problems in their work area, many changes in layout will already have occurred, and much waste will be removed, clearing the way for the more advanced techniques of continuous flow and kanban.

5.4 SELECT AND PREPARE THE TEAM

5.4.1 Select the Team Leader

How-to Steps

After choosing the area and the problem focus for the workshop, the workshop leader and process owner must identify the team leader. The team leader leads the team conducting the workshop, and works with the workshop leader to provide input to the sponsor and process owner about who should be on the team. He or she also helps prepare for the workshop, creates schedules, gathers the needed supplies and instruments, and follows all workshop activities, removing obstacles and helping with documentation and reporting. The leader keeps the team on target, ensuring that they meet the workshop objectives. Team leaders should be selected far enough ahead of the workshop so that they can rearrange their schedules to make leading the workshop their top priority.

Leaders must have participated in a kaizen workshop before leading one, but they do not have to know how to solve the problems on which the workshop is focused. Their role is to support the team members in finding solutions—to facilitate an open exchange of ideas and to ask the questions that spur creative problem solving among the team members. A team leader may work in the area chosen for the workshop, but team leaders should also be encouraged to gain experience by leading teams in other areas of the facility. See Figure 5.4 for the qualities a good team leader should have.

5.4.2 Prepare the Team Leader

Team leaders will need to become familiar with the A3T charter so that they understand the goals and objectives of the workshop, the healthcare service production requirements, and the expectations of team members. Information from past workshops should be shared with the team leader, such as past problems encountered and gains achieved. The team

Qualities of a Good Team Leader

A good team leader should have the following qualities and experience:

1. Previous leadership experience; not necessarily management experience, it can be experience as a scout leader, soldier, mother, etc.

2. Experience as a leader or coleader in other kaizen workshops; must have at least participated in a previous workshop

3. An awareness of the methods of Lean healthcare

4. A good leadership style (that is, Socratic versus dictatorial or didactic)

5. An understanding of participative management

6. Be able to be firm but fair, aggressive *and* friendly

7. Be able to take control when necessary

8. Be willing to be out on the floor for the event, not out of reach in the office

Figure 5.4 The qualities of a good team leader.

leader should also be given information about what to do in an emergency, safety rules related to the area, what to do when things bog down, how to handle personality conflicts, and where to access needed data. In addition to selecting the team members, the leader has a number of responsibilities and activities before, during, and after the workshop. Figure 5.5 lists some of the workshop leader and team leader responsibilities, and how they support one another.

5.4.3 Select the Team Members

How-to Steps

The team leader's first responsibility is to work with the workshop leader and process owner to select team members. The team members are the people who actually conduct the kaizen workshop. All team members must be able to participate in the entire workshop, with no exceptions. If they are unable to attend any portion of the workshop, they should not be on the team.

There should be at least six and no more than twelve people on the team. Most should be clinicians and staff members

Kaizen Workshop Roles and Responsibilities

Workshop Leader (WSL)

- *Accountable to sponsor*

- *Responsible for workshop flow, target metric achievement, and quality of final product*

Planning

- Attend all planning meetings.

- In coordination with team leader (TL), facilitate weekly planning meetings beginning 4 weeks prior to the workshop. (Refer to 4-3-2-1 checklist, Figure 5.8.)

- In coordination with TL, responsible for preworkshop gemba (gemba is a Lean term derived from a Japanese word meaning "the real place"; it refers to the actual place where healthcare processes are performed) observations and data collection.

- Work with sponsor to establish workshop target metrics.

During the Workshop

- Ensure adherence to kaizen week standard work and agenda items and allotted times.

- Assist TL with setting up the daily agenda.

- Work with TL to divide kaizen team into subteams by grouping idea summary sheets (see Figure 6.8) into categories/projects.

- With TL, report out to process owner (PO) and sponsor on Monday of workshop to review targets, and on Tuesday and Wednesday to review progress/summary of the day's work.

- Obtain/coordinate support services resources as needed.

- Take lead in working with any team member exhibiting disruptive or negative behavior, or who is otherwise significantly impacting progress of rest of team; escalate to management or sponsor if needed.

- In coordination with TL, create Kaizen Action Bulletin (see Figure 7.3).

- Create final report-out presentation.

- Collect all final versions of documents created during the workshop and save to USB drive for hand off to PO and Kaizen Promotion Office (KPO).

Figure 5.5   Team leader and workshop leader responsibilities.

After the Workshop

- Huddle with TL, PO, and sponsor to discuss any concerns or issues regarding implementation.

- Hand off final documents (USB drive) to PO and KPO.

Team Leader (TL)

- *Accountable to workshop leader*

- *Responsible for managing and facilitating the team to deliver the final product*

Planning

- Attend all planning meetings.

- In coordination with WSL, facilitate weekly planning meetings beginning 4 weeks prior to the workshop. (Refer to 4-3-2-1 checklist, Figure 5.8.)

- In coordination with WSL, responsible for preworkshop gemba observations and data collection.

During the Workshop

- Responsible for hands-on facilitation of kaizen workshop.

- Work with WSL to divide kaizen team into subteams by grouping idea summary sheets (see Figure 6.8) into categories/projects.

- Work with WSL to create a daily agenda.

- Ensure the kaizen team continuously focuses on the Lean process and principles.

- Demonstrate effective facilitation by not "telling" the team solutions or answers; rather, coach and ask questions to help them get to their own solutions.

- Support team on gemba.

- Escalate issues and barriers to WSL, as appropriate.

- Support WSL in reporting out to sponsor and PO on Monday of workshop to review targets and on Tuesday and Wednesday to review progress/summary of the day's work.

After the Workshop

- Huddle with WSL, PO, and sponsor to discuss any concerns or issues regarding implementation.

Figure 5.5 (continued)

from the workshop area. These people know the operations and processes and can answer questions about the area. But it is critical that at least three members be drawn from outside the workshop area. These people will bring new perspectives. Also, try to include a patient on the team. It may be difficult to identify a patient that can commit to being present for the entire five-day workshop. Try to find a volunteer or staff person in another department that has been a frequent or recent patient in the area.

Key Point

Team members must be chosen for their ability to work together and also because they understand and support the potential of the kaizen workshop. Those who complain or belittle the potential will slow down or even block success, especially for the first few workshops you implement. Once successful workshops have been led, these naysayers may become your strongest participants, but in the beginning they should be left off of workshop teams. The workshop leader, the sponsor, and the process owner can help the team leader identify those who will make strong team members.

Improvement methodologies work best when partnered with positive attitudes. See Figures 5.6 and 5.7 for attitudes that will get in the way of kaizen and Lean healthcare. These need to be addressed on an organizationwide scale. The most effective way is to give team members real empowerment in these workshops and then to communicate their positive results to the whole medical center.

TAKE FIVE

Take five minutes to think about these questions and to write down your answers:

1. Would you like to be included in a kaizen workshop team? Why?
2. What qualities do you think make a good team member?
3. Who do you work with that has the qualities of a good team leader?
4. Who actually conducts the kaizen workshop?

Taboo Phrases

When talking about improvements, never say the following:

1. "Do it yourself!"

2. "We can't get costs any lower."

3. "This is good enough."

4. "I'm too busy to do it."

5. "That's not part of my job."

6. "I can't do it."

7. "It won't work in healthcare."

8. "It's your responsibility, not mine."

9. "We're already doing fine. We don't need to change."

Figure 5.6   Taboo phrases for kaizen and Lean production.

Ten Arguments That Need to Be Addressed

1. Kaizen won't do any good!

2. It sounds like a good thing, but we still don't want to do it!

3. Looks good on paper, but …

4. Costs are already as low as they can possibly get!

5. But we've already been doing things that way!

6. We don't want people looking over our shoulders and telling us what to do!

7. We can't lower costs any more without lowering quality!

8. Everything is going just fine now. Why change it?

9. That's a lousy idea! We already tried that twenty years ago!

10. Look, we understand this stuff better than anybody (so don't tell us what to do).

Figure 5.7   Ten arguments against kaizen that need to be addressed.

5.5 OTHER PREPARATIONS

5.5.1 Prepare the Area

Preparation of the workshop area can make or break a kaizen workshop. Without meticulous preparation, there can be no successful kaizen. This is usually the responsibility of the process owner. The area chosen for the workshop should be uncluttered; otherwise the workshop will be spent removing junk and cleaning up the area. If the area is too messy, the team leader and workshop leader should discuss the need for starting with 5S, either before the workshop or as the focus of the workshop itself.

New Tool

Preparation for a kaizen workshop begins weeks in advance. *The Kaizen Workshop Planning Checklist, or "4-3-2-1" Checklist* (see Figure 5.8) captures the many activities required to make the workshop a success: logistics, team needs, communications, and financial and support personnel.

Remember, it is essential to ensure that the sponsor and process owner communicate about kaizen activity:

1. Senior leaders should send an announcement (from the top of the organization).
2. Post the schedule and describe what will happen.
3. Communicate daily.
4. Involve the union.
5. Show before and after pictures.
6. Thank maintenance and others who support kaizen activity.
7. Don't stop communicating after the workshop is done.

5.5.2 Prepare Supplies, Equipment, and Support People

If the needed supplies, equipment, and support people are not in place, the workshop will fail. Make sure there is sufficient lighting and ventilation in the area. Security may need to be notified of the workshop so that they will be alerted to any unusual activities that will be occurring.

Key Point

Support departments such as Engineering, Environmental Services, Facilities, and IT need to be put on alert. The team may need personnel to respond quickly to help make a change, for example to move equipment or computers or install shelves.

Team members and assigned support personnel should be easily identified during the workshop—give them team hats, shirts, vests, or pins to wear, so that everyone in the medical center knows who they are and what is happening.

New Tool

The team leader needs to prepare a supply kit for the workshop. These supply kits are described in Chapter 6. A *Supplies and Equipment Checklist* such as the one in Figure 5.9 can help keep track of your supplies and equipment needs.

5.5.3 Gather Background Information

Consider how the workshop will affect the other shifts in that area. Is it possible to have someone from each shift represented on the team so that changes can be communicated easily to all shifts after the workshop? If healthcare services must continue to be provided, understand what the requirements will be and how to ensure effective completion of the workshop without stalling those requirements. Also consider the workshop's possible impact on the processes upstream and downstream of the workshop area. Will the workshop eliminate major bottlenecks or work in process, or will it cause them to shift to another area? Will WIP inventory still be needed in the area after the workshop? If so, where will it be stored? Or is this one of the issues the team must solve during the workshop?

Gather the information you will need to answer questions that may arise during the workshop. Time can be wasted searching for data in order to make decisions about takt time (the rate of patient demand), process requirements, and case mix. Use the *Background Information List* (Figure 5.10) to gather the information you may need.

New Tool

5.5.4 Schedule the Workshop

A typical kaizen workshop requires 5½ hours on Monday, 8 hours on Tuesday, Wednesday, and Thursday, and 3–4 hours

rona consulting group

Kaizen Workshop (KW) Planning Checklist

	Enter start date of Kaizen Workshop (Monday):		4/22/13

	☑	Complete by	Task

- 4 weeks prior

	☐	03/29/13	Identify workshop target area, processes, and products
	☐	03/29/13	Identify sponsor(s), process owner, workshop leader, and team leader
		03/29/13	Ensure management buy-in and commitment
	☐	03/29/13	Announce workshop dates to management team
	☐	03/29/13	Schedule planning meeting for next week to include:
			* sponsor(s) *process owner *workshop leader (WSL) *team leader (TL) *KPO staff
	☐	03/29/13	Complete value stream map
	☐	03/29/13	Schedule sponsors for kick-off (Mon am), mid-week report outs (Tues & Wed pm),
			and closing comments (after Fri formal report out)
	☐	03/29/13	Identify whether physician(s) need to be on team & work to free their schedules

- 3 weeks prior

	☐	04/05/13	Attend planning meeting and determine:
	☐	04/05/13	* Specific boundaries of KW (use A3). ie, "process begins at __ and ends at __;
			customers and suppliers are __".
	☐	04/05/13	* Which specific operations will be within the boundaries
	☐	04/05/13	* Workshop objectives
	☐	04/05/13	* What equipment will be needed
	☐	04/05/13	* Which jobs will be evaluated
	☐	04/05/13	* What support services must be notified to be available "on call" during week
			(eg Engineering, Environmental Services, Facilities, etc)
	☐	04/05/13	* Communications plan for target area staff to involve and prepare them for KW
	☐	04/05/13	* Critical success factors (how will the Process Owner know the KW is a success?)
	☐	04/05/13	* Draft list of workshop participants
	☐	04/05/13	Obtain copies of facilities layouts of target areas (8.5"x11")
	☐	04/05/13	Videotape the process flow
	☐	04/05/13	Conduct detailed analysis of area to identify barriers and issues that must be
			resolved before the KW can proceed
	☐	04/05/13	Develop action plan for each barrier/issue to be completed before workshop date
	☐	04/05/13	Start identifying opportunities for improvement (refer to A3 for priorities)
	☐	04/05/13	Using a Target Sheet, identify initial 5-day improvement metrics
	☐	04/05/13	Develop draft agenda for the 5 days of the KW
	☐	04/05/13	Book a room for the workshop team close to the workshop gemba
	☐	04/05/13	Identify and contact workshop participants
	☐	04/05/13	Contact support services identified during planning meeting to obtain names/
			pager numbers of on-call personnel for KW week
	☐	04/05/13	Have Process Owner schedule staff mtg for next week

(a)

Figure 5.8   A sample kaizen workshop planning, or 4-3-2-1 checklist.

on the fifth day, Friday. The workshop leader and process owner need to double check with everyone involved in the workshop to be sure that they have cleared their calendars for the scheduled dates. This is particularly important in the case of busy doctors, who may require notice up to ten weeks prior to the kaizen workshop. Remember, 100 percent participation is required of all team members the entire week. It is essential that they and their managers understand this. No meetings—no leaving early or arriving late because of other work issues.

	☑	Complete by:	Task:
- 2 weeks prior	❑	04/12/13	Send notification letter to participants
	❑	04/12/13	Communicate to support services and all people in selected work area:
			* Date of workshop
			* Purpose of workshop
			* Process to be followed
			* Expected payoff
			* Role & responsibilites of people selected to participate
			* Role & responsibilites of people NOT selected to participate
	❑	04/12/13	Involve key workshop participants in planning & preparation (those who will be instrumental in achieving improvements)
	❑	04/12/13	Scheduled staff meeting occurs, to explain objectives, agenda, what to expect during week, and expected results
	❑	04/12/13	Ensure process owner posts flip chart(s) in work area to capture concerns/questions
	❑	04/12/13	Decide how communication will happen during week between participants and rest of dept staff, including across shifts
	❑	04/12/13	Print Participant Mauals
- 1 week prior	❑	04/19/13	Finalize KW agenda, including start and end times for each day (may need to flex depending on the operating hours of the gemba) and time for Fri formal report out
	❑	04/19/13	Finalize Target Sheet. Ensure it aligns with A3
	❑	04/19/13	Communicate (if possible meet) with all workshop participants to reinforce understanding of purpose of week, the week's activities, their roles and responsibilities during the week, and responsibilities for communication back to rest of department
	❑	04/19/13	Discuss with Process Owner and any supervisors what follow-up activities will be required after the week, and their responsibilities to support these (example: implementation of Kaizen Action Bulletin; coaching & training all staff on new processes/standard work; change management activities)
	❑	04/19/13	Ensure availability of computer & projector for Monday teaching session
	❑	04/19/13	Transport to workshop room: * Participant Manuals, * KW supply kit, * Copies of KW agenda, * Flip charts & stands, * Nameplates
	❑	04/19/13	Prepare room for teaching day - arrange chairs, desks, etc.
	❑	04/19/13	Post data on wall (VSM and any other relevant info or data)
During KW	❑	04/22/13	Have VSMaps available and copies of A3 on A3 paper
	❑	04/22/13	Prepare room for education with projector and flip charts
	❑	04/22/13	Prepare flip chart agenda every morning before team arrives
	❑	04/22/13	First activity of every morning must be Hansei
	❑	04/22/13	Sponsor meeting 4:30 - 5:00 M,T,W
Friday of KW	❑	04/26/13	Prep room for Final Report Out presentation with projector and microphone
	❑	04/26/13	Immediately after report-out, 15' huddle with Sponsor, Process Owner, and Workshop Leader to ensure smooth handoff of Kaizen Action Bulletin & to identify specific support needed from QDS or Sponsor
	❑	04/26/13	Collect idea forms & data forms completed during week & add to Book of Knowledge (eg Time Observ. Forms, Standard Work Sheets, SWCS, % load charts, Std Wk Instruc.
	❑	04/26/13	Upload Final Report Out presentation to QDS website
	❑	04/26/13	Collate evaluations

(b)

Figure 5.8 (continued)

The dates for the workshop have probably been set from the beginning by the workshop leader and process owner, but now that the area has been prepared, the team leader and workshop leader can work out a more detailed agenda. Figure 5.11 shows a typical schedule for a one-week workshop to implement continuous flow.

Supplies Checklist

Lean Forms:

☐ Time Observation Sheet

☐ Standard Work Sheet

☐ Standard Work Combination Sheet

☐ Percent Load Chart

☐ Standard Work Instruction Sheet

☐ Standard Work Tracking Form

☐ Standard Work Validation Checklist

☐ Red Tags

☐ Red Tag Logs

☐ 5S: 5 Point Standardization Checklist

☐ 5S: 5 Point Standardization Summary

☐ 5S: Job Cycle Chart

☐ 5-minute 5S

Office Supplies:

☐ Pens

    ☐ Ball Point – black

    ☐ Sharpie – black, red, blue, green

    ☐ White Board – black, red, blue, green

    ☐ Flip Chart – black, red, blue, green

    ☐ Highlighter – yellow, pink, orange, green

☐ Pencils

☐ Tape

    ☐ Masking, white

    ☐ Cellophane

    ☐ Floor Marking

☐ White-Out

Figure 5.9 A sample supplies and equipment checklist.

Tools:

☐ Clipboards

☐ Rulers

☐ Stopwatches

☐ Calculators

☐ Flip Chart

    ☐ Additional flip chart paper

Equipment:

☐ Label Maker

    ☐ Additional cartridges

☐ Laminator

    ☐ Laminating sheets

☐ PC

    ☐ Microsoft Word

    ☐ Microsoft Excel

    ☐ Microsoft PowerPoint

    ☐ Color Printer

        ☐ Additional ink cartridges

        ☐ White printer paper

        ☐ Colored printer paper

Figure 5.9 (continued)

5.6 SUMMARY

The first step in planning for a kaizen workshop is to choose where it will be conducted. You can choose several areas where you would like to start and compare the merits of each. In order to have a big impact right away, choose an area that is deluged with WIP, that has activities that occur all over the medical center, that has a significant bottleneck or other major hindrance to healthcare service production flow, or where everything is a mess. Choose an area where most

Background Information List

1. Historical or expected patient demand or patient census—by day, week, month

2. Value stream map of the process to be improved

3. Layout map of the area

4. The case mix of different diagnoses and/or acuities in the clinical process to be improved

5. Names of clinicians and staff members, their job descriptions, and required levels of licensure

6. Clinic hours of operation and shift change schedules

7. Copies of relevant nursing protocols

8. Copies of relevant organizational policies and procedures

9. CMS or Joint Commission regulations and guidelines

10. Articles about any relevant evidence-based practices

11. Par levels or amounts of WIP of supplies needed to allow normal healthcare service production requirements to be met during and after the event

Figure 5.10 Background information list.

of the clinicians and staff members are ready and willing to make changes, where clinicians and staff members have already been cross-trained or have been exposed to kaizen workshops before, and with which most of the employees are familiar.

Once the area has been selected, the focus for the kaizen workshop must be decided. In selecting a focus for the kaizen workshop, several things need to be considered. Has 5S been conducted there? Has standard work been implemented to stabilize healthcare service production? Should that be the focus of the first workshop in this area or do you want to implement 5S more gradually before conducting the workshop? Should standard work be the initial focus of improvement? The complexity involved and the length of time needed to prepare for your kaizen workshop depends on the problem you choose to improve or the implementation

Workshop Schedule

Monday	11:00 a.m.	Train participants in Lean healthcare concepts and methods.
	1:30 p.m.	Review value stream map, A3T, and targets for the workshop.
	2:30 p.m.	Go to gemba to observe and document additional process wastes.
	4:30 p.m.	Review progress and scope with workshop sponsor and process owner.
	5:00 p.m.	First day ends—focal points of improvement activity are well understood.
Tuesday	8:00 a.m.	Prioritize improvement ideas and form improvement subteams.
	9:30 a.m.	Go to gemba: Observe the process; conduct small tests of change.
	4:30 p.m.	Review progress and scope with workshop sponsor and process owner.
	5:00 p.m.	Second day ends—process documentation is complete, more tests of change are planned.
Wednesday	8:00 a.m.	Return to gemba to continue observations and tests of change.
	4:30 p.m.	Review progress and scope with workshop sponsor and process owner.
	5:00 p.m.	Third day ends—most tests of change completed.
Thursday	7:00 a.m.	Conduct additional tests of change as required.
	8:00 a.m.	Draft new standard work instructions and plan in-service training.
	2:30 p.m.	Complete new process documentation and final presentation.
	3:30 p.m.	Practice presentation.
	5:00 p.m.	Fourth day ends—process documentation and presentation are complete.
Friday	8:00 a.m.	Rehearse presentation again and complete workshop evaluations.
	9:30 a.m.	Make final presentation to the organization.
	10:00 a.m.	Hand off documents to workshop sponsor, process owner, and KPO.
	10:30 a.m.	Workshop ends.

Figure 5.11 A typical workshop schedule.

you wish to lead. These also determine the length of the workshop itself.

The first challenge of kaizen is to understand how to identify waste. First you examine what is; you pay close attention to what you do that is value-added and what you do that is not. And then you experiment with ways to eliminate the things you do that are not value-added. Problem solving is the heart of kaizen. It begins with one idea. And it never ends.

Continuous flow, mistake-proofing, pull systems, and *kanban* are advanced Lean methods that have grown from the simple beginnings of identifying waste in order to eliminate overproduction, excess inventory, and unnecessary transport from value-added operations and processes. Kaizen workshops can focus on implementing these advanced techniques and they are often used for this purpose, but it is wise to implement simpler approaches to identifying and eliminating waste first. 5S starts you off on the right foot. It's a perfect tool for bringing a team of clinicians and staff members together and allowing them to focus on their own areas first. Standard work is an excellent way to follow 5S. Not only does standard work stabilize the production of healthcare services, it eliminates a great deal of waste and sets the stage for gathering the data required to implement more advanced Lean healthcare methods including continuous flow and mistake-proofing.

After choosing the area and the problem focus for the workshop, the team leader must be identified. The *team leader* leads the team conducting the workshop; he or she helps choose the team members, creates the daily schedules, gathers the needed supplies and instruments, and follows all workshop activities, removing obstacles and helping with documentation and reporting.

The *team members* are the people who actually conduct the kaizen workshop. They must be chosen for their ability to work together and because they understand and support the potential of the kaizen workshop. There should be at least six and no more than twelve people on the team. Most should be clinicians and staff members from the workshop area, but outsiders can be useful members, too.

Preparation of the workshop area can make or break a kaizen workshop. The area chosen should be uncluttered; otherwise the workshop will be spent removing the junk and cleaning up the area. If the needed supplies, equipment, and support people are not in place, the workshop will fail. Support departments will need to be notified of the workshop so that they will be alerted to the unusual activities that will be occurring and ready to provide assistance if needed.

Consider how the workshop will affect the other shifts in that area. Also consider the workshop's possible impact on the upstream and downstream processes of the workshop area. Gather the information you will need to answer questions that may arise during the workshop. Time can be wasted searching for data in order to make decisions about takt time, process requirements, and case mix. Use the Background Information List to gather the information you may need. Then create the detailed schedule for the workshop.

5.7 REFLECTIONS

Now that you have completed this chapter, take five minutes to think about these questions and to write down your answers:

- What did you learn from reading this chapter that stands out as particularly useful or interesting?
- Do you have any questions about the topics presented in this chapter? If so, what are they?
- What additional information do you need to fully understand the ideas presented in this chapter?

Chapter 6

Phase Two

Run the Kaizen Workshop

The area has been selected and prepared. Key personnel are on hand for needed support, and supplies have been gathered for ready use. The focus for the kaizen workshop has been selected and an agenda has been carefully thought out. It is now time for the workshop itself.

6.1 ORIENTATION

How-to Steps

The kaizen workshop begins with an orientation session conducted by the workshop leader (see Figure 6.1). The session should include a brief overview of Lean methodology, as an introduction for new participants and a review for any team members that have some experience with kaizen.

6.1.1 Introduce the Team and Assign Roles

In the breakout room you have arranged for the team meetings, have the team leader and team members introduce themselves and describe their jobs, what they do outside of work, and what they know about kaizen workshops. Explain the workshop leader and team leader roles.

Then discuss the team member roles. If appropriate, assign someone on the team to shoot video and/or take digital photos before, during, and after the workshop. Through playback, video documentation can help you analyze operations and determine opportunities for improvement. These visual records can also make valuable additions to your presentation at the end of the workshop. Photos are especially useful when performing

Figure 6.1 Orienting the team.

5S improvements. However, if you plan to shoot videos or take photos of areas or processes, be sure that you check your facility's policies beforehand. Introduce the maintenance or other support liaison and identify a team member who will work with the support team as needed to plan equipment moves or other needs that will arise during the workshop.

6.1.2 Introduce the Workshop Objectives and Procedures

Introduce the objectives of the workshop. What will the team be expected to achieve? How will the workshop be conducted? Tell the team about any additional training they may receive before the work begins, or briefly review any training that has already occurred and give the team time to ask questions.

Key Point

Team members will be required to participate without interruption throughout the workshop. The breakout room should be quiet, with refreshments and meals provided and restroom facilities nearby. No cell phone or job-related interruptions should be allowed. All workshop kit items and flip charts, white boards, and markers should be provided in

Figure 6.2 Where does kaizen happen?

the room where the team will gather to analyze data, share ideas, take breaks, and create the presentation. However, the majority of the workshop time will be spent in the focus area. In fact, *all key players should know that their kaizen time will be best spent on the floor—not behind a desk* (see Figure 6.2).

Key Point

6.1.3 Distribute Team Supply Kits and Resources

The team receives a kit of supplies for use during the workshop. The team kit should include paper for writing and sketching, pens, pencils, erasers, tape, Post-it® notes, felt-tip markers in several colors, stopwatches, and any other supplies they may need to illustrate ideas and work out solutions. Each member also receives a notebook of work forms needed in the workshop, an overview of the process, and the workshop agenda.

After reviewing the team kits and notebooks, the team leader describes the shared resources, listed in the following text, that have been gathered to support the team in their analysis of the processes in the area and in their improvement activities.

The shared resources include the following items:

1. Value stream maps, flow charts, and process sheets
2. The A3T or team charter that has sanctioned the improvement activity
3. Medical center layouts and workshop area layouts
4. Photos of the area
5. Cycle times of current processes (cycle time is the amount of time it takes for a clinician or staff member to complete an operation or sequence of tasks in a healthcare process)
6. Patient demand requirements or takt time
7. Current staff and support personnel
8. Defect and rework data
9. Case mix
10. Average numbers of setups per day
11. List of current problems
12. Current improvement projects being considered
13. Goals and objectives
14. Safety issues and rules
15. Healthcare organization and union rules

6.1.4 Conduct Lean Healthcare Training

When an organization begins its Lean journey, most of the initial training is focused on senior leaders before improvement activity begins in earnest. People in the organization who are close to daily operations often know very little about Lean healthcare or kaizen. Therefore, a typical kaizen workshop includes a brief training session in basic Lean concepts and Lean tools. In addition to the overview of Lean concepts and methodologies, the team will need to understand any specific tools and methods they will use to meet the objectives of the workshop. This training will continue through the first day as the workshop proceeds, and normally includes a *waste walk* focused on discovering examples of the seven wastes (see Chapter 2, Figure 2.1) in the work area chosen as the focus of the week's improvement activity. Additional training in specific tools, notably the running time study, is conducted on a *just-in-time* basis throughout the kaizen week. If 5S is the focus of the work-shop, then training will occur at the beginning of each day as you move to the next segment of implementation. Even if people have been through training sessions in these methods prior to the workshop, you will want to review the tools now so that the team has a fresh perspective of how to proceed.

6.1.5 Set Ground Rules

As the team begins working together, have them set ground rules about how they will interact during the week. Ask them: "What bothers you in meetings?" Examples of ground rules include:

- No side conversations
- Must raise hand before speaking
- Put all cell phones on vibrate

Also, make sure everyone understands any constraints that may exist related to moving equipment, changing medical center layout, or spending money to implement solutions.

Good teamwork behaviors will make the workshop more enjoyable as well as productive. Review the ten kaizen work-shop rules with everyone (see Figure 6.3). Ask for comments and ask for everyone's agreement to the rules.

Review the agenda for the workshop until everyone is clear about what will be expected. It will be hard work and every-one must understand what to expect and that they must work together to make a great workshop.

TAKE FIVE

Take five minutes to think about these questions and to write down your answers:

1. What are the three kaizen workshop rules that you like best?
2. What training in Lean healthcare methods have you already had?
3. Do you know the cycle time of your own operation?

Ten Kaizen Workshop Rules

1. There is no rank among team members—one person, one vote.

2. Keep an open mind to change.

3. Change is good, more change is better.

4. Maintain a positive attitude.

5. Don't blame anyone for anything.

6. Respect one another.

7. There is no such thing as a dumb question.

8. Plans are only good if they can be implemented. Plans succeed only if the gains are sustained.

9. There is no substitute for hard work.

10. Just do it!

Figure 6.3 Attitudes for success.

6.2 UNDERSTAND THE CURRENT SITUATION IN THE GEMBA

After the orientation and training, the team needs to understand the current situation in the gemba—that is, in the real place where healthcare happens, on the floor, in the focus area. It is essential for all team members to physically observe the processes of healthcare in order to discover the root causes of delays and defects and to understand what types of countermeasures may actually work.

Depending upon your workshop focus, you may or may not take all of the steps and use all of the tools discussed here. The point is to do whatever you have to do to fully observe, record, and understand the baseline situation.

6.2.1 Observe the Selected Area and Gather Data

How-to Steps

Review the layout and, if available, the *before* photos of the workshop area with the team in the breakout room, and then take the team to the area to observe it and walk the process flow.

Gather data to perform a case mix analysis. Group patients by common processes and operations and then in descending volume order. Select a case using a Pareto analysis, which will help you choose an improvement target that will give you the most return for your efforts.

Gather quality data, defect rates, and the sources of defects. Walk the route that patients travel and measure travel distance. Calculate square feet occupied by the current process. Investigate setups—how many and how often; identify bottlenecks and what causes them. Note current staffing. Determine all support persons assigned to the area. Use *Time Observation Forms* (discussed in Section 6.2.3) and *Standard Work Sheets* (see Figures 6.4a and 6.4b) to collect and plot the data.

New Tool

In workshops focused on implementing 5S, standard work, quick setup times, or continuous flow, baseline data collection will be done to serve those objectives. Refer to the other books in this Lean Tools for Healthcare Series for details about the methods, instruments, and measures needed to implement the various Lean healthcare improvements in a kaizen workshop.

6.2.2 Review the Value Stream Map

Prior to your workshop, you should have created a value stream map or perhaps another type of process map. This helped you to identify areas of waste that might be eliminated through kaizen activity. Typically a kaizen workshop will not focus on all of the operations identified in the process that you have mapped. The workshop will focus on a subset of operations or perhaps on a single operation (see Figure 6.5).

New Tool

To establish and maintain the proper focus for the event, review your map before you begin the data collection, and complete a *Pre-Kaizen Target Sheet* (see Figure 6.6). Here are some tips for completing the target sheet:

How-to Steps

1. Before the kaizen workshop, enter metrics in the Baseline column. You will enter the revised metrics on days 1 through 3 and at the end of the workshop in the respective columns.

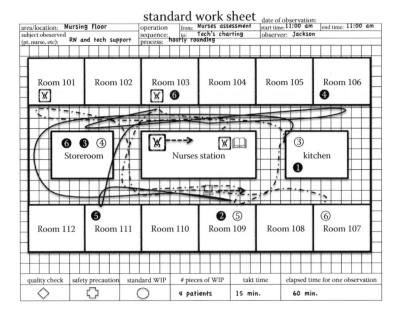

(a)

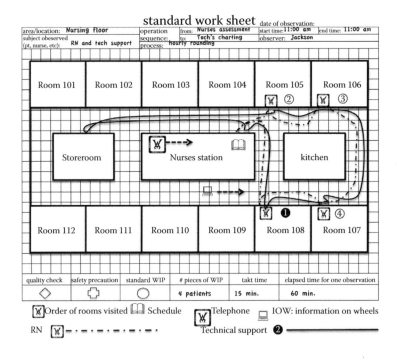

(b)

Figure 6.4 Standard work sheets for a nursing floor, before and after kaizen.

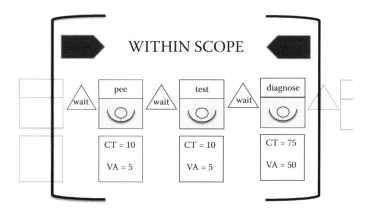

Figure 6.5 A targeted subset of operations—not the whole value stream—is chosen as the focus area.

2. Never enter TK or TBM ("to come" or "to be measured") as a metric. Either use data from simulations or, if there is no new data to report, carry forward the baseline metric.

3. For any metrics that will be tracked, add a specific target metric (to replace the percentage) in the Target column.

4. Recalculate the percent change at every remeasurement using the most recent value, and list it in the Percent Change column. It is always expressed as a percentage change from baseline [(Baseline − Most Recent Value)/Baseline], not the percentage change from the most recent measurement. A positive value indicates success.

5. Here are recommendations on how to calculate each measure:

- Space: square footage of floor space used.
- Inventory: monetary value of supplies kept in the area, regardless of whether they can be returned for credit.
- Walking distance: number of linear feet walked by clinicians and staff members in the process. (Note, this also represents time spent!)
- Parts travel distance: number of linear feet traveled by a patient or a part during the process.
- Lead time: total number of minutes elapsed in the process, from beginning to end.
- Quality (% defects): percentage of defects in the process.

Target Progress Report and Results Sheet

rona consulting group

Team Name: _Kaizen Workshop #5_
Department: _Interventional Radiology_
Product/Process: _IR Procedure Admit_

Date: _22-Apr_
TAKT Time: _20 minutes_
Team Leader: _A. K._

Measures:		Baseline	Target	Day 1	Day 2	Day 3	Final	Percent Change
Space (sq footage)			>= 50%					
Inventory (dollars)			>= 50%					
Walking Distance (feet)			>= 50%					
Parts Travel Distance (feet)			>= 50%					
Lead Time (minutes)		_45'_	_20'_					
Quality (% Defects)	Numerator (# defects)	_2_	_0_					
	Denominator (sample size)	_20_	_n/a_					
	Percentage	_10%_	_0%_					
Productivity Gain (mins of operator time) Aggregate/convert to FTEs			>= 50%					
Environmental, Health & Safety (5S) Levels 1 - 5		_1_	_3_					
Set-Up (minutes per operation)			<= 9 min					
Other								

Remarks: _Lead Time: From patient check-in to admission complete_
Defects: % of time admit documentation is incomplete
5S: 5S level in admit area.

© 2010 rona consulting group

Figure 6.6 A sample pre-kaizen target sheet.

- Productivity gain: difference between the annualized labor required to complete a process before kaizen and the labor required after kaizen.
- Environmental health and safety (5S): levels 1 to 5, as assessed with standard 5S audit tools. (The final score is the lowest of the scores assigned to Sort, Set in order, and Shine.)
- Setup: total number of minutes elapsed between the end of the last good procedure and the beginning of the next.
- Other: used to capture gains (usually financial gains) that don't fit into the other metrics.

6.2.3 Do Time Studies of All Operations

New Tool

If the workshop focus is 5S, set up red tag areas and follow the steps of the 5S process. Otherwise, the next step is to do time studies of the relevant operations. Talk to the clinicians and staff members before you do this and discuss the reasons you are observing them. Fill in your calculations on the *Time Observation Form* (Figure 6.7). Compare or calculate takt time and calculate lead time. Document any unique process or handling required. Note setup frequencies and times. Create a Standard Work Sheet of the flows in the area. The Standard Work Sheet is also called a *spaghetti diagram* because when you accurately depict all the movement that typically occurs, the mass of lines resembles spaghetti. (You can refer to the *Standard Work for Healthcare* book in this series for information about how to use the tools mentioned throughout Section 6.2.)

TAKE FIVE

Take five minutes to think about these questions and to write down your answers:

1. What would a spaghetti diagram of the area you work in now look like? Draw one.
2. How would you do a time study of your area?

---

time observation form

area/location: Dermatology	date of observation: 3/5/10
subject observed: RN	start time: 9:15am
process: Intake/assessmt	observer: T. Brown

		observation time						
step no.	description of operation	observations					Mode (most freq. occurring) task time	remarks
		1	2	3	4	5		
1	Walk to front desk/registration area	0:00 / 0:09	0:00 / 0:11	0:00 / 0:10			0:10	
2	Retrieve pt's chart & intake forms	0:09 / 0:07	0:11 / 0:08	0:10 / 0:07			0:07	
3	Walk to waiting area	0:16 / 0:05	0:19 / 0:05	0:17 / 0:04			0:05	
4	Call pt name x2	0:21 / 0:06	0:24 / 0:04	0:21 / 0:04			0:04	
5	Wait while pt approaches	0:27 / 0:29	0:28 / 0:30	0:25 / 0:15			0:30	
6	Greet pt	0:56 / 0:04	0:58 / 0:05	0:40 / 0:06			0:05	
7	Walk to Tx room, set down ppwk, sit	1:00 / 0:18	1:03 / 0:19	0:46 / 0:17			0:18	
8	Open chart / review	1:18 / 0:07	1:22 / 0:08	1:03 / 0:09			0:08	
9	Interview: ask pt questions, write in chart	1:25 / 3:10	1:30 / 3:14	1:12 / 3:18			3:14	
10	Realize missing a form: walk to front desk to retrieve	4:35 / 0:10	4:44 / 0:10	4:30 /			0:10	3rd obs: was not missing form
11	Look for form/find	4:45 / 0:07	4:54 / 0:07	4:30 /			0:08	
12	Walk back to room / sit	4:52 / 0:10	5:01 / 0:10	4:30 /			0:10	
13	Continue interview	5:02 / 2:30	5:11 / 2:26	4:30 / 2:15			2:26	
14	Walk to sink	7:32 / 0:03	7:37 / 0:03	6:45 / 0:03			0:03	
15	Wash hands / put on gloves	7:35 / 0:14	7:40 / 0:15	6:48 / 0:16			0:15	
16	Walk to pt	7:49 / 0:03	7:55 / 0:03	7:04 / 0:03			0:03	
17	Examine wound/lesions, talk to pt	7:52 / 0:24	7:58 / 0:25	7:07 / 0:30			0:25	
18	Walk to sink	8:16 / 0:03	8:23 / 0:03	7:37 / 0:04			0:03	
19	Remove gloves / wash hands	8:19 / 0:10	8:26 / 0:11	7:41 / 0:12			0:11	

Figure 6.7   A sample time observation form.

6.3 DEVELOP IMPROVEMENTS

How-to Steps

Now that the team has thoroughly observed the current situation and has a clearer understanding of the actual situation, they can begin to identify improvement priorities and actually develop and test improvements.

6.3.1 Generate and Capture Improvement Ideas

New Tool

When the team returns from gemba, team members will use *Idea Summary Sheets* to draw a picture of their personal

Idea Summary Sheet

Employee / Area	Problems	Measures Taken	Results
Incomplete med records from Pre-Reg	Documents missing on day of service	• Held MD's accountable for doc submission • Begin chart assembly earlier • QC process in place	↑ Chart complete by 30% prior to date of service

Remarks: _Charts are to be complete 48° prior to date of service._

Notes:_____

Figure 6.8 A sample idea summary sheet.

visions for improvement (see Figure 6.8). Ask each team member to draw at least three ideas. Everyone needs to draw, not just write, their ideas. By requiring people to both write and draw their ideas, idea summary sheets help people articulate and communicate complex ideas quickly and effectively. The team must do idea generation silently—no discussion.

TAKE FIVE

Take five minutes to think about these questions and to write down your answers:

1. What are the seven types of waste? Can you identify any of these in your own work area? What causes this waste?
2. What could you do to eliminate them?

6.4 FACILITATE TEAMWORK

Keep in mind that, as teams implement ideas or run into problems, the workshop leader may need to reprioritize several times during the week. Teams that are too large will not function well. In particular, it will be difficult for everyone on a large team to participate effectively. During the course of a five-day workshop, this can give rise to significant frustration, especially among doctors and executives.

To ensure high participation levels, break large teams into small groups or subteams. Make sure that each subteam has its own appropriate leader. Right-size teams throughout the week to ensure that small group interaction is always lively.

The workshop leader should round on all subteams at least twice a day to make sure that subteam leaders keep their teams focused and that teams have the resources they need. Team leaders should stay in gemba with their subteams. Subteams must all convene to report to each other both at midday and at the end of each day. There is often overlap among their activities so they must stay updated on what the other teams are working on.

The role of the workshop leader is to coach, not to solve problems. Don't give in to the temptation to be a star player. Use open questions to provoke Lean thinking! Note: If subteams need support departments called in, they must make those requests through the workshop leader. All such requests must be coordinated to avoid duplicate and/or inappropriate or unnecessary requests from multiple team members.

Keep the energy level high. Listen carefully to the tone of team and subteam interactions. Is it harmonious? Discordant? Is everyone involved? You can easily tell when people are engaged or disengaged. Be proactive. Respond appropriately with helpful questions to discover the causes of prolonged discord or silences. Remind team members of the expectations you set on Monday.

6.5 TEST IDEAS AND IMPLEMENT THE NEW PLAN

During the kaizen week, subteams will test their improvement ideas in gemba. The testing of ideas should begin no later than Wednesday morning. All tests should be completed by Wednesday evening, although subteams may come early to the workshop on Thursday morning if there are additional tests to run.

If appropriate and consistent with your facility's policy, try to document the area using camera and/or video before you change it. A picture says a thousand words. Especially for 5S activities, a pair of before and after pictures, taken from exactly the same spot and at the same angle, says volumes. Before and after pictures of improved processes are the very best forms of evidence.

The workshop leader should notify the maintenance or other support staff when you are ready to change the floor or make other changes that require support. Clean out the area of focus, leaving only what is required for the new process. Mark the floor as needed. If equipment needs to be moved, make a detailed layout with instructions for maintenance so that they can make the moves during the night if necessary. Note any areas needed for WIP, setups, instruments, and other support functions in the process.

Figure 6.9 shows an example from an OR kaizen workshop in the Ambulatory Care Unit (ACU) before and after 5S.

Storage room, before and after 5S

Figure 6.9 A storage area, before and after kaizen.

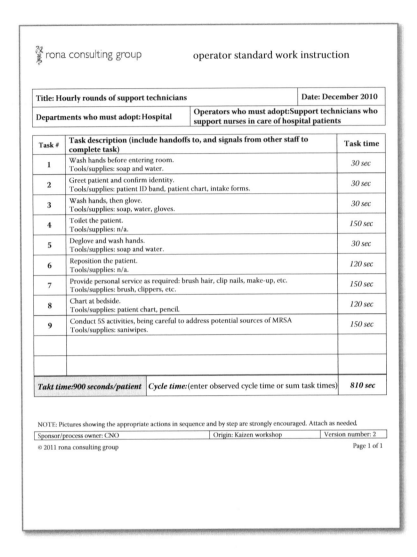

rona consulting group   operator standard work instruction

Title: Hourly rounds of support technicians		Date: December 2010
Departments who must adopt: Hospital	Operators who must adopt: Support technicians who support nurses in care of hospital patients	

Task #	Task description (include handoffs to, and signals from other staff to complete task)	Task time
1	Wash hands before entering room. Tools/supplies: soap and water.	30 sec
2	Greet patient and confirm identity. Tools/supplies: patient ID band, patient chart, intake forms.	30 sec
3	Wash hands, then glove. Tools/supplies: soap, water, gloves.	30 sec
4	Toilet the patient. Tools/supplies: n/a.	150 sec
5	Deglove and wash hands. Tools/supplies: soap and water.	30 sec
6	Reposition the patient. Tools/supplies: n/a.	120 sec
7	Provide personal service as required: brush hair, clip nails, make-up, etc. Tools/supplies: brush, clippers, etc.	150 sec
8	Chart at bedside. Tools/supplies: patient chart, pencil.	120 sec
9	Conduct 5S activities, being careful to address potential sources of MRSA Tools/supplies: saniwipes.	150 sec
Takt time: 900 seconds/patient	Cycle time: (enter observed cycle time or sum task times)	810 sec

NOTE: Pictures showing the appropriate actions in sequence and by step are strongly encouraged. Attach as needed.

Sponsor/process owner: CNO	Origin: Kaizen workshop	Version number: 2
© 2011 rona consulting group		Page 1 of 1

Figure 6.10 A sample standard work instruction sheet.

After implementing their improvement ideas, subteams observe the work being performed in the new way.

1. Use the Time Observation Form to record new cycle times.
2. Document the new standard using the Standard Work Instruction template.
3. Communicate, communicate, communicate.

Then, encourage the team to find more ways to make the work safer, easier, quicker, and more consistent. Do this again and again. Kaizen is never finished; you just run out of time.

Train the clinicians and staff members in the new process and test it until it is running smoothly, at the improved level. Observe and record new cycle times. Note any problems and check for safety issues. Is there enough WIP at the needed locations? Calculate all savings from the eliminated waste: clinician or staff member motion, part conveyance, square footage taken up by the new process, throughput time, and so on. Complete all process analysis sheets for the new process, including the *Standard Work Instruction Sheet* (Figure 6.10), so that you can compare it to the old process in your report.

New Tool

6.6 DEVELOP NEW STANDARDS

Set new targets and define the measures for the new process. Make your targets as concrete and/or as quantifiable as possible. Record all new data. Complete as much of the implementation as you possibly can within the workshop time frame. What cannot be implemented should be recorded on a follow-up sheet for completion after the workshop. The workshop leader will be responsible for assigning and seeing that these items are completed in a timely fashion.

TAKE FIVE

Take five minutes to think about these questions and to write down your answers:

1. With all you have learned, do you think you would like to participate in a kaizen workshop?
2. What areas in your medical center do you think should be the focus of kaizen workshops first?

6.7 SUMMARY

The kaizen workshop begins with an orientation meeting. Introduce the team, assign roles, and introduce the workshop objectives and procedures. Team members will be required to participate without interruption throughout the workshop and the majority of the workshop time will be spent in the focus area. All key players should know that their kaizen time will be best spent on the floor—not behind a desk. Distribute supplies and resources. Make sure everyone understands any constraints that may exist related to moving equipment, changing medical center layout, or spending money to implement solutions. Review the ten kaizen workshop rules with everyone. Review the agendas for the workshop until everyone is clear about what will be expected. Though some training may have been conducted before the workshop, a brief introduction or review will be needed now for the team to understand the instruments and methods they will use to meet the objectives of the workshop.

After the orientation and training, the team needs to understand the current situation in the focus area. Take the steps necessary to fully observe, record, and understand the baseline situation. Review the layout and the before photos (if available) of the workshop area with the team in the breakout room, and then take the team to the area to observe it and walk the flow. Observe the area, gather data, complete the Pre-Kaizen Target Sheet, and review the value stream map of the area so that you can analyze the process. This will prepare you to identify areas of waste that might be eliminated. Do time studies of all operations. Talk to the clinicians and staff members before you do this and discuss the reasons you are observing them. Identify and record the wastes you find in the area. Record the magnitude of waste you find. Search for the root causes of the problem and ask the five whys. Work with the clinicians and staff members to find solutions. Ask, "What would this process look like if it were free of waste?"

With current improvement targets in mind, brainstorm to create new ideas, using the *Idea Summary Sheets*. Think out of the box! Meet with clinicians and staff members to collaborate on the new ideas. Test the improvement ideas as much as possible before changing the layout. Then implement the new plan. Train the clinicians and staff members and test the new process. Observe and record data for the new process and compare it to the old process. Set new targets and define the measures for the new process.

6.8 REFLECTIONS

Now that you have completed this chapter, take five minutes to think about these questions and to write down your answers:

- What did you learn from reading this chapter that stands out as particularly useful or interesting?
- Do you have any questions about the topics presented in this chapter? If so, what are they?
- What additional information do you need to fully understand the ideas presented in this chapter?

Chapter 7

Phase Three

Report and Follow-Up

At key points during the workshop (normally on Tuesday and Wednesday afternoons, after the team is dismissed), the workshop leader and team leaders report current daily progress to workshop sponsors, who provide feedback and guidance to the team. The workshop leader makes sure that these report meetings start and stop on time.

Once implementation is complete and all data for the new process has been recorded, it is time to prepare the presentation of results and to celebrate.

7.1 PRESENTATION

7.1.1 Prepare a Presentation of All Data and Workshop Results

How-to Steps

On the last day of the workshop, all team members participate in presenting the results of their kaizen activity to senior management. Typically the workshop leader will coordinate the preparation of the presentation and choose the information and materials to be included.

The presentation includes actual documentation, including standard work sheets, time observation forms, idea summary sheets, the new floor layout and spaghetti diagram, standard work instruction sheets for each clinician or staff member and/or station, illustrations that explain the improvements, and before and after videos or digital photos, if available. The team should begin creating this documentation early in the week. Quantify your success in terms that are important to your business, such as costs avoided or reduced lead times. Did you meet or exceed your goal? If you came close, what else needs to happen

Workshop Leader Checklist for Report Out

☐ Process is serving patients at takt time with zero defects.

☐ Takt time calculations are correct.

☐ Cost–benefit analysis meets finance department standards.

☐ Idea Summary Sheets are compiled.

☐ Time Observation Forms and Percent Load Charts are compiled.

☐ New layouts are documented on Standard Work Sheets.

☐ New Standard Work Instructions are completed.

☐ In-service training for clinicians and staff is scheduled.

☐ 30-day Kaizen Action Bulletin is complete.

☐ Slide presentation completed, including team photo and thanks to all involved.

☐ List made of recommended future improvements.

☐ Final reflection on the week's activities with the team completed.

☐ Workshop evaluations are completed.

☐ Final run-through of presentation is complete.

☐ All necessary documentation is complete and transferred to USB drive.

Figure 7.1 A sample workshop leader checklist for report out.

to meet the goal? The workshop leader can use the checklist in Figure 7.1 to get ready for the presentation.

On the morning of the last workshop day before the final report, the workshop leader should ask each team member for a brief description of what they learned from the workshop personally. Complete the *Workshop Evaluation Form* (Figure 7.2).

New Tool

7.1.2 Present the Results

Key Point

On the afternoon of the next to last day (usually Thursday afternoon) and again on the morning of the final day, the team

Workshop Evaluation Form

Date: Organization: Workshop Leader:
Name: Location: Team Leader:
Phone: Service Line: Sponsor:
E-mail: Team Name: Process Owner:

1. What was your overall impression of the workshop?

   _____

   _____

2. What would you change about the workshop to make it more useful?

   _____

   _____

3. Would you like to participate in another workshop, yes or no, and tell why?

   _____

   _____

4. Did the workshop accomplish all that it could, or was there more that could have been done?

   _____

   _____

5. How were you treated? Could you give your opinions freely?

   _____

   _____

		Poor								*Great*	
6.	Please rate the Workshop Leader	1	2	3	4	5	6	7	8	9	10
7.	Please rate the Team Leader	1	2	3	4	5	6	7	8	9	10
8.	Quality of training material	1	2	3	4	5	6	7	8	9	10
9.	Usefulness to the organization	1	2	3	4	5	6	7	8	9	10
10.	Usefulness in your current work	1	2	3	4	5	6	7	8	9	10

Additional comments please:

_____

_____

_____

Figure 7.2   A sample workshop evaluation form.

should gather to rehearse the presentation. The team leader should always start the presentation. The workshop leader is responsible for advancing the slides as the team members speak sequentially about their selected set of slides. Time everyone's part and assess who is going on too long. Help team members refine or enhance their comments to effectively convey the story of the week. The presentation should not run more than twenty minutes. Each team member participates in some way; even the presentations should be a team effort.

7.1.3 Cover Ideas That Have Not Been Fully Implemented

New Tool

Improvement ideas that your team was not able to complete during the week are recorded on a kaizen action bulletin (see Figure 7.3). Responsibility and a due date are assigned for each unfinished item. Completion is expected within thirty days. Only one name may appear in the Responsibility column for any single item.

Although many may help, ultimate responsibility for completion of the bulletin lies with the process owner (whose name appears at the top right of form). Kaizen action bulletins should be completed by all subteam leaders and should be included as part of their report on Friday.

7.1.4 Build the Book of Knowledge

Before the workshop concludes, the workshop leader collects all documents created during the workshop. These may include standard work sheets, time observation forms, percent load charts, standard work instructions, idea summary sheets, A3Ts, and before and after photos. These documents form the core of your "book of knowledge" and track the evolution of your standard work. They are the vital record of your organizational learning. The book of knowledge should also include the workshop leader's final report, a simple report that outlines key changes in bullet-point format. The documents should be handed to the representatives from your KPO (Kaizen Promotion Office).

7.1.5 Circulate and Display Results

Circulate results to top management and anyone else who should have them. Display results in a central area for people to read at their leisure. The workshop leader should make hard copies of the team presentations, and publicize the good results to the healthcare organization. The workshop leader will have invited the appropriate people to the presentation. The logistics of the presentation and any celebration planned are the workshop leader's responsibility also.

7.2 FOLLOW-UP

Key Point

Follow-up is necessary to reap the full benefit of kaizen. *The workshop is, in some ways, never over. Results must be monitored and improvements continually made.* There are always many things left to complete. The real success of the workshop will be measured only after all the recommendations have been implemented.

The sponsor and process owner should meet at least once a week for four weeks following the workshop and review the status of each kaizen action bulletin item. This is to ensure that items are completed within thirty days, that changes are being sustained, and that the proposed countermeasures are having the desired impact.

The workshop leader will review the results with the executive team and plan the next steps, including subsequent workshops to be held. Were there any surprises or failures? Were the objectives met? How can future workshops be improved?

Evaluation forms should be reviewed by management and used to inform plans for future workshops. The next workshop leader should check the results of this workshop to make sure all the follow-up items were completed. Do not start the next workshop until the last one has been finished.

Clinicians and staff members on the lines impacted by the workshop should be contacted no more than a week after the workshop for feedback on the changes that have been made. Make a list of their suggestions or complaints and give feedback to the process owner. Clinicians and staff members should

Kaizen Action Bulletin

Department:

Date:

Team Name:

Owner:

Item #	Problem	Countermeasure	Responsibility	Date	Status
					A P / C D
					A P / C D
					A P / C D
					A P / C D
					A P / C D

Figure 7.3 A kaizen action bulletin form.

participate in weekly meetings to measure the new system and consider their ideas for correcting flaws in the original design.

New Tool

Results of the new process should be tracked and posted daily on run charts (simple charts that plot a process value over time). After thirty days, publish the results and compare them to the old standards to show the accumulated savings to date. Use the *Post-Kaizen Target Sheet* (see Figure 7.4) to track numeric progress of certain metrics related to kaizen improvements. On this sheet, you'll record the 30-, 60-, and 90-day results of the metrics you tracked during the kaizen workshop (see Chapter 6, Figure 6.6).

Track the savings weekly for a year. Remember, whatever you track will improve. If clinicians and staff members were moved to other areas because of the workshop, make sure that everyone knows what they are doing and that none were released or laid off. Thanks to the kaizen training, all clinicians and staff members involved should be valuable players anywhere they are placed.

Remind everyone that kaizen is more than a workshop—it never ends. Kaizen is now the way you do your work.

7.3 SUMMARY

On the last day of making improvements, team members must rehearse the presentation before they can adjourn. On the morning of the final day, the team should gather to rehearse the presentation. Each team member participates in some way; even the presentations should be a team effort. Complete the *Workshop Evaluation Form* before the celebration begins. Circulate results to top management and to anyone else who should have them. Display results in a central area for people to read at their leisure.

The workshop is, in some ways, never over. Results must be monitored and improvements continually made. There are always many things left to complete. Use the *Kaizen Action Bulletin* to record and track to-do items. The real success of the workshop will be measured only after all the recommendations have been implemented.

Target Progress Report and Results Sheet

rona consulting group

Team Name: _Kaizen Workshop #5_   Date: _26-Apr_
Department: _Interventional Radiology_   TAKT Time: _20 minutes_
Product/Process: _IR Procedure Admit_   Team Leader: _A. K._

Measures:		Baseline	Target	Day 1	Day 2	Day 3	Final	Percent Change
Space (sq footage)			>= 50%					
Inventory (dollars)			>= 50%					
Walking Distance (feet)			>= 50%					
Parts Travel Distance (feet)			>= 50%					
Lead Time (minutes)		45'	20'					
Quality (% Defects)	Numerator (# defects)	2	0	3	1	0	0	
	Denominator (sample size)	20	n/a	20	20	20	20	
	Percentage	10%	0%	15%	5%	0%	0%	100%
Productivity Gain (mins of operator time) Aggregate/convert to FTEs			>= 50%					
Environmental, Health & Safety (5S) Levels 1 - 5		1	3	1	1	2	3	50%
Set-Up (minutes per operation)			<= 9 min					
Other								

Remarks: _Lead Time: From patient check-in to admission complete_
    Defects: % of time admit documentation is incomplete
    SS: SS level in admit area.

© 2010 rona consulting group

Figure 7.4   A sample post-kaizen target sheet.

Clinicians and staff members on the lines impacted by the workshop should be contacted no more than a week after the workshop for feedback on the changes that have been made. Results of the new process must be posted daily. Use the *Post-Kaizen Target Sheet* to publish results, compare them to the old standards, and show the accumulated savings to date at 30, 60, and 90 days after the workshop. Continue to track the savings weekly for a year. Remember, whatever you track will improve.

Remind everyone that kaizen is more than a workshop—it never ends. Kaizen is now the way you do your work.

7.4 REFLECTIONS

Now that you have completed this chapter, take five minutes to think about these questions and to write down your answers:

- What did you learn from reading this chapter that stands out as particularly useful or interesting?
- Do you have any questions about the topics presented in this chapter? If so, what are they?
- What additional information do you need to fully understand the ideas presented in this chapter?

Chapter 8

Reflections and Conclusions

8.1 SUMMARY OF STEPS FOR CONDUCTING A KAIZEN WORKSHOP

The following sections briefly summarize the key steps for conducting a kaizen workshop.

8.1.1 Phase One: Plan and Prepare

Select a workshop leader—will you use an outside consultant?

Communicate to the entire healthcare organization the plans for a kaizen workshop.

Select an area:

- Use the Kaizen Workshop Area Selection Matrix to determine priorities for areas to be selected.
- Create or review existing value stream maps.

Select a problem for improvement.

Select the team leader or coleaders and prepare them.

Select the team members.

Prepare the area.

- Gather needed supplies and equipment.
- Notify necessary support departments and people.
- Get needed background information.

Schedule the workshop.

8.1.2 Phase Two: Run the Kaizen Workshop

Orientation:

- Introduce the team and assign roles.

- Introduce the workshop objectives and procedures.
- Distribute team supply kits and resources.
- Conduct needed training and set ground rules.

Understand the current situation in the gemba:

- Observe the selected area and gather data.
- Review the value stream map.
- Do time studies of all operations (or set up areas for 5S implementation).

Make the improvements:

- Develop improvement ideas.
- Test ideas and implement the new plan.
- Develop new standards.

8.1.3 Phase Three: Report and Follow-Up

Present the results of the kaizen workshop to the health-care organization:

- Prepare a presentation of all data and workshop results.
- Complete the Workshop Evaluation Form.
- Present the results and circulate them to top management and anyone else who should have them.
- Build the book of knowledge by submitting all documents and the final report to the Kaizen Promotion Office.
- Display results in a central area for people to read at their leisure.

Celebrate the completion of the workshop.

Follow-up:

- Use the Kaizen Action Bulletin to assign follow-up tasks and make sure they are completed.
- Get feedback from the clinicians and staff members in the workshop area.
- Document and continue to track results using the Post-Kaizen Target Sheet.
- Consider next steps, next kaizen workshops, and the next Lean training that is needed.

8.2 REFLECTING ON WHAT YOU HAVE LEARNED

Key Point

An important part of learning is reflecting on what you've learned. Without this step, learning can't take place effectively. That's why we've asked you to reflect at the end of each chapter. And now that you've reached the end of the book, we'd like to ask you to reflect on what you've learned from the book as a whole.

Take ten minutes to think about the following questions and to write down your answers.

- What did you learn from reading this book that stands out as particularly useful or interesting?
- What ideas, concepts, and techniques have you learned that will be most useful to you during kaizen workshops? How will they be useful?
- What ideas, concepts, and techniques have you learned that will be least useful during kaizen workshops? Why won't they be useful?
- Do you have any questions about kaizen? If so, what are they?

8.3 OPPORTUNITIES FOR FURTHER LEARNING

Here are some ways to learn more about kaizen:

- Find other books, videos, or training materials on this subject. Several are listed in the Appendix.
- If your healthcare organization is already conducting kaizen workshops, visit other departments or areas to see how they are applying the ideas and approaches you have learned about here.
- Find out how other companies have conducted kaizen workshops. You can do this by reading magazines and books about Lean healthcare implementation, and by attending conferences and seminars presented by others.

8.4 SUMMARY

Kaizen is more than a series of techniques. It is a fundamental approach to improving the healthcare process. We hope this book has given you a taste of how and why this approach can be helpful and effective for you in your work.

Appendix

FURTHER READING

Rona Consulting Group & Productivity Press, *5S for Healthcare* (New York: Productivity Press, 2009).
> Restates the universal concept and practices of 5S—creating a clutter-free and organized workplace—in a language that speaks to healthcare providers and staff.

Rona Consulting Group & Productivity Press, *Standard Work for Lean Healthcare* (New York: Productivity Press, 2012).
> Explains how to apply the powerful Lean tool of *standard work* to increase patient safety and reduce the cost of providing healthcare services.

Mark Graban, *Lean Hospitals: Improving Quality, Patient Safety, and Employee Satisfaction, 2nd edition* (New York: Productivity Press, 2012).
> *Lean Hospitals* explains why and how Lean can be used to improve quality, safety, and morale in a healthcare setting. Graban highlights the benefits of Lean methods and explains how Lean manufacturing staples such as Value Stream Mapping can help hospital personnel identify and eliminate waste, effectively preventing delays for patients, reducing wasted motion for caregivers, and improving quality of care.

Naida Grunden, *The Pittsburgh Way: Improving Patient Care Using Toyota Based Methods* (New York: Productivity Press, 2008).
> Author Naida Grunden provides a hopeful look at how principles borrowed from industry can be applied to make healthcare safer, and in doing so, make it more efficient and less costly. The book is a compilation of case studies from units in different hospitals around the Pittsburgh region that applied industrial principles successfully, making patients safer and employees more satisfied.

USEFUL WEBSITES

Lean Blog, http://www.leanblog.org/.
> A blog founded by author Mark Graban about Lean in factories, hospitals, and the world around us.

John Grout's Mistake Proofing Center, http://www.mistakeproofing.com.

Shingo Prize-winner John Grout's collection of three websites devoted to poka-yoke (mistake proofing), a key technique for kaizen and Lean operations generally. An entire website within the center is devoted to mistake-proofing applications in healthcare.

Rona Consulting Group, http://www.ronaconsulting.com.

The official website of Series Editor Thomas L. Jackson and his partners at the Rona Consulting Group.

Productivity Press, http://www.ProductivityPress.com.

The website of Productivity Press, where you can order the books listed in the Further Reading section of this Appendix, among many other works about Lean healthcare, Lean manufacturing, total quality management (TQM), and total productive maintenance (TPM).

Index

Printed and bound by PG in the USA

USA2019PGIL